THE RIGHT STUFF;

THE RIGHT STUFF;

Ian Hay

www.General-Books.net

Publication Data:

Title: The Right Stuff
Author: Ian Hay
General Books publication date: 2009
Original publication date: 1910
Original Publisher: Houghton Mifflin company
Subjects: Biography Autobiography / General
Biography Autobiography / Historical
Biography Autobiography / Women
Biography Autobiography / Personal Memoirs
History / General
Juvenile Fiction / General
Juvenile Fiction / Business, Careers, Occupations

CONTENTS

1

SECTION 1

PREFACE

I Consider it my duty, as author of this volume, to buttonhole the reader on the threshold of the story, and caution him. This done, he goes inside under no illusions and at his own risk.

The Right Stuff was originally written for English and Scottish readers, the author (an individual of a retiring and unsanguine disposition) never having considered the possibility of his work falling into the hands of a larger and less parochial public. Under these circumstances American readers are warned that: –

1. The hero is a Scotsman, and he and his relatives occasionally revert to a dialect and idiom which, despite the advent of Mr. Harry Lauder, is not yet so universally prevalent on these shores as it doubtless deserves (and expects) to be.

2. Many of the incidents are of a particularly local and British character. They depict the habits and customs of the average upper-class Briton in a fashion which characteristically takes for granted the rather large proposition that the rest of the civilised world handles such things as electioneering and game-shooting hi precisely the same manner as John Bull. Consequently the narrative will be found frequently to diverge frpm the paths ofbald and obvious platitude into the trackless . byways of technical incomprehensibility.

3. The scene is laid entirely hi Great Britain. The Englishman likes to read about localities he knows, so that if the villain abducts the heroine in a motor-car in the centre of London – say Piccadilly Circus – the reader may feel sure of his ground while he accompanies the hero in a headlong pursuit in another car down Regent Street or Shaftesbury Avenue. *(N. B.* No such incident occurs in this book.)

For all these blemishes the author expresses regret. In extenuation he urges that although the subject-matter may be lacking in originality, the style open to criticism, and the syntax shaky, the spelling and punctuation are (thanks to the printer and proof-reader) unexceptionable.

He also ventures to believe that men and women and children – especially children – are much the same all the world over, and that a simple study of human nature, set down without malice, illustrated by pictures of the common joys and sorrows of life, and interwoven with the ancient and unoriginal but never-dying theme of the way of a man with a maid, may meet with as sympathetic and indulgent an audience on the west side of the Atlantic as it has done on the east.

Ian Hay.

Edinburgh, January, 1910.

CHAPTER ONE.

OATMEAL AND THE SHORTER CATECHISM.

The first and most-serious-but-one ordeal in the life of Robert Chalmers Fordyce – so Robert Chalmers himself informed me years afterwards – was the examination for the Bursary which he gained at Edinburgh University. A bursary is what an English undergraduate would call a " Schol." (Imagine a Scottish student talking about a " Burse "!)

Robert Chalmery Fordyce arrived in Edinburgh pretty evenly divided between helpless stupefaction at the sight of a great city and stern determination not to be imposed upon by the inhabitants thereof. His fears were not as deep-seated as those of Tom Pinch on a similar occasion, – he, it will be remembered, suffered severe qualms from his familiarity with certain rural traditions concerning the composition of London pies, – but he was far from happy *t* He had never slept away from his native hillside before; he had never seen a town possessing more than three thousand inhabitants; and he had only once travelled in a train.

Moreover, he was proceeding to an inquisition which would decide once and for all whether he was to go forth and conquer the world with a university education behind him, or go back to the plough and sup porridge for the rest of his life. To-morrow he was to have his opportunity, and the consideration of how that opportunity could best be gripped and brought to the ground blinded Robin even to the wonders of the Forth Bridge.

He sat in the corner of the railway carriage, passing in review the means of conquest at his disposal. His actual stock of scholarship, he knew, was well up to the required standard: he was as letter perfect in Latin, Greek, Mathematics, and Literature as hard study and remorseless coaching could make him. Everything needful was in his head – but could he get it out again ? That was the question. The roaring world in which he would find himself, the strange examination-room, the quizzing professors – would these combine with his native shyness to seal the lips and cramp the pen of Robert

ChalmersFordyce ? No – a thousand times no! He would win through! Robert set his teeth, braced himself, and kicked the man opposite.

He apologised, attributing the discourtesy to the length of his legs – he stood about six feet three – and smiled so largely and benignantly, that the Man Opposite, who had intended to be thoroughly disagreeable, melted at once, and said it was the fault of the Company for providing such restricted accommodation, and gave Robert *The Scotsman* to read.

Robert thanked him, and, effacing himself behind *The Scotsman,* – though, for all the instruction or edification that his present frame of mind permitted him to extract from that coping-stone of Scottish journalism, he might as well have been reading the Koran, – returned to his thoughts. He collated in his mind the pieces of advice which had been bestowed upon him by his elders and betters before his departure. In brief, their collective wisdom came to this: –

His father had bidden him –

(a) To address all professors with whom he might come in contact as " Sir" ;

(6) To arrive at the Examination each morning at least five minutes before the advertised time;

(c) To refrain from lending money to, or otherwise countenancing the advances of, persons of insinuating address who would doubtless accost him in the streets of Edinburgh.

The Dominie had said –

" When in doubt, mind that practically everything in an examination governs the subjunctive.

" If there is a *viva voce,* be sure and speak up and give your answers as though you were sure of them. They may be wrong, but on the other hand they may be right. Anyway, the one thing the examiners will not thole is a body that dithers.

"Take a last keek at that Proposition – they *may* call them Theorems, though – about the Square on the Hypotenuse. It hasn't been set for four years.

" If you are given a piece of Greek Testament to translate, for mercy's sake do not be too glib. Dinna translate a thing until you are sure it is there. They have an unholy habit of leaving out a couple of verses some place in the middle, and you're just the one to tumble head-first into the *lacuna.* (I ken ye, Robbie!)

"And whatever ye do, just bear in mind it's your only chance, and *grup* on tae it! *Post estoccasio calva,* laddie ! And dinna disappoint an auld man that has taught ye all he kens himsel'!"

Much of his mother's advice was of a kind that could not be expressed so concisely, but two salient items remained fixed in Robert's mind : –

" If ye canna think o' the richt word, pit up a bit prayer.

" For ony sake see that your collar is speckless a' the time."

Robert's first impressions of Edinburgh were disappointing. Though extensive enough, the city was not so great or so imposing as he had expected. It was entirely roofed with glass, – a provision which, though doubtless advantageous in wet weather, militated against an adequate supply of sunlight and fresh air. The shops, of which Robin had heard so much, were few in number; and the goods displayed therein (mainly food and drink, newspapers and tobacco) compared unfavourably in point of variety with those in the window of Malcolm M'Whiston, the "merchant" at home. The inhabitants all appeared to be in a desperate hurry, and the noise of the trains, which blocked every thoroughfare, was deafening. Robert Chalmers was just beginning to feel thoroughly disappointed with the Scottish capital, when it occurred to him to mount a flight of stairs which presented itself to his view and gave promise of a second storey at least. When he reached the top he found he had judged Edinburgh too hastily. There was some more of it.

His horizon thus suddenly enlarged, Robert Chalmers Fordyce began to take in his surroundings. He now found himself in a great street, with imposing buildings on one side and a green valley on the other. On the far side of the valley the ground ran steeply upward to an eminence crowded thickly with houses and topped by a mighty castle.

The street was alive with all sorts of absorbingly interesting traffic; but for the present Robert was chiefly concerned with the Cable Cars. It was upon one of these majestic vehicles, which moved down the street unassisted by any apparent human or equine agency, that he had been bidden to ride to his destination. He was not to take the first that came along, nor yet the second – they went to various places, it seemed; and if you were taken to the wrong one you had to pay just the same – but was to scan them until he espied one marked " Gorgie." This would carry him down the Dairy Road, andwould ultimately pass the residence of Elspeth M'Kerrow, a decent widow woman, whose late husband's brother had " married on " a connection of Robert's mother. Here he was to lodge.

At first sight the cars appeared to be labelled with nothing but Cocoa and Whisky and Empire Palaces of Varieties Open Every Evening; but a little perseverance discovered a narrow strip of valuable information painted along the side of each car. The first that caught our friend's eye was " Pilrig and Braid Hills Road." That would not do. Then came another – " Murrayfield, Haymarket, and Nether Liberton." Another blank! Then, " Marchmont lload and Churchill." Foiled again, Robert was beginning to feel a little sceptical as to the actual existence of the Dairy Road, when a car drew up opposite to him labelled "Pilrig and Gorgie." It was going in the right direction too, for his father had warned him that his destination lay to the west of the town; and you can trust a Scotsman to know the points of the compass with his eyes shut. (They even talk of a man sitting on the north or south side of his own fireplace.)

Robert clambered on to the top of this car, and presently found himself confronted by agentleman – splendid in appearance but of homely speech – who waved bundles of tickets in his face, and inquired tersely –

"Penny or tippeny? or transfair?"

"I am seeking the Dairy Road," said Robert cautiously.

"Which end o't?"

" I couldna say."

" Ca' it a penny," said the conductor.

Robert, with the air of a man who has beaten down his opponent to the lowest possible figure, produced the coin from his pocket. (It was just as well that the man had not demanded a larger sum, for Robert's more precious currency was concealed in a place only accessible to partial disrobement.) The gorgeous man carelessly snapped a ticket out of one of the bundles, and having first punched a hole in it with an ingenious instrument that gave forth sounds of music, handed it to Robert in exchange for the penny. He was a saturnine man, but he smiled a little later when Robert, mindful of the fate of his railway-ticket at the last station but one, airily attempted to give up his car-ticket in similar fashion on alighting at the end of the journey.

The greater part of the next four days wasspent by our friend in an examination-room, into which we, more fortunate, need not attempt to follow him. Robert diligently answered every question, writing at the foot of each sheet of his neat manuscript, " More on the next page," in case the examiner should be a careless fellow and imagine that Robert had finished when he had not. Robert was not the man to leave anything to chance, or to such unsafe abbreviations as P. T. O.

Outside the examination-room he devoted most of the time that he could spare from preparation for the next paper to a systematic exploration of Edinburgh. He did the thing as thoroughly as possible, for he knew well that he might never spend four days in a large town again.

He began by climbing the Calton Hill. He remained at the summit quite a long time, constructing a rough bird's-eye plan of the streets and buildings below him; and having descended to earth, proceeded on a series of voyages of discovery.

He regarded the exterior of Parliament House with intense interest, for he was a debater by instinct and upbringing. St Giles' he passed by without enthusiasm – he was a member of the Free Kirk – and St Mary's Cathedral struckhim as being unduly magnificent to be the property of such a small and pernicious sect as the Episcopalians. The Post Office and other great buildings struck him dumb; and he hastened past the theatres with averted eyes, for he had it upon unimpeachable authority that the devil resided there.

He knew no one in Edinburgh save Elspeth M'Kerrow. However, he made another friend – to wit, one Hector MacPherson, a gigantic Highland policeman, who controlled the traffic with incredible skill at a place where several ways met. The said Hector stood beneath the shadow of a great lamp-post, and whenever a vehicle drove past one side of him, Hector relentlessly called it back and made it go on the other. Their acquaintance began with the entire efface- ment of Robert's features by the palm of Hector's hand, which was suddenly extended across the thoroughfare for traffic - regulating purposes, with the result that Robert, who was plunged in thought at the time, ran his nose right into the centre of it. The ejaculation to which each gave vent at the moment of impact revealed to both that they were from the same part of the country, and thereafter Hector MacPherson became Eobert's adviser - in - chiefthroughout his stay in Edinburgh. Indeed, Robert used Hector as the starting-point for all his excursions, and whenever he became hopelessly lost in the wilds of the Grassmarket or the purlieus of Morningside, he used to ask his way back to his mentor's pitch and make a fresh start. We shall hear of Hector again.

The foolhardy feat of entering a shop Robert did not attempt until his very last day in Edinburgh, and then only because he was absolutely compelled to do so by the necessity of executing a commission for his sister Margaret – the purchase of half a yard of ribbon.

It is true that the same ribbon could have been obtained at home from Malcolm M'Whiston or a travelling packman, Hmt Margaret was determined to have it from Edinburgh; aud she was particularly emphatic in her injunctions to Robert to see that the folk in the shop stuck a label on the parcel, " with their name printed on, and a picture of the shop and a'."

On Saturday morning, then, Robert approached the establishment which he had chosen for the purpose. After a careful reconnaissance he discovered that it possessed several doors. Here was a poser. Which would be the ribbon door ? Supposing he entered the wrong one and foundhimself compelled to purchase a roll of muslin or a wash-hand-stand? With natural acumen he finally selected a door flanked by windows containing lace and ribbon; and waiting for a moment when the surging crowd was thickest, attempted to slip in with them. He got safely past a hero in a medal-sown uniform, but immediately after this encountered an imposing gentleman in a frock-coat, who asked his pleasure. Robert inquired respectfully if the gentleman kept ribbon. The gentleman said " Surely, surely!" and Robert's modest requirements were thereupon sent ringing from a throat of brass into the uttermost recesses of the establishment, and he himself was passed, hot-faced, along the fairway until he reached the right department. Here his tongue clove to the roof of his mouth, and the siren behind the counter, with difficulty stifling her amusement, was reduced to discovering his needs by a process of elimination.

" What will I show you ? "

No answer.

"Ladies' gloves?"

A shake of the head.

"Handkerchiefs?"

Another shake.

"Stockings?"

Another shake, accompanied by a deepening of complexion.

Well – ribbon?"

" Aye, that's it," replied Robert, suddenly finding his voice (which, by the way, rather re- fiembled the Last Trump). " Hauf a yaird – one inch wide – satin – cream !" he roared mechanically.

He received the small parcel, and furtively fingering the money in his pocket, asked the price.

" Two-three, please," replied the damsel briskly.

How Robert thanked his stars that he had some cash in hand! But what a price 1 All that for a scrap of ribbon! It seemed sinful; but he laid two shillings and threepence on the counter. Greatly to his alarm, the young woman behind it, who up to this point had kept her feelings under commendable control, suddenly collapsed like a punctured balloon on to the shoulder of her nearest neighbour – there being no shop-walkers about – and expressed a wish that she might be taken home and buried. Finally she recovered sufficiently to push Robert's two shillings back across the counter and to place his threepence in a mysterious receptacle which she thrust into a hole in thewall, from which it was ejected with much clatter a minute later; and on being opened proved to contain what the dazed Robert at first took for a half-sovereign, but which he ultimately discovered, when he had abandoned the still giggling maiden and groped his way out into the street, to be a bright new farthing.

The same day he returned to his home; but he did not reach it without one more adventure, a slight one, it is true, but not without its effect upon his future.

The train was over-full, and Robert ultimately found himself travelling in company with nine other passengers, seven of whom were suffering from that infirmity once poetically described by an expert in such diagnoses as " a wee bit drappie in their een." The exception was a gentleman in the far corner, accompanied by a most lovely young lady, upon whom Robert gazed continuously with an admiration so absorbing and profound that it took him some little time to realise, shortly after the commencement of the journey, that the rest of the company were indulging in a free fight all over the compartment, and that the lady was clinging in terror to her escort. Robert was of considerable service in restoring order, and found his reward in the eyes of thelady, who thanked him very prettily. Her husband had the sense not to offer Robert money, but gave him his card, and said in a curious, stiff, English way that he hoped he might be of service to him some day. They got out at Perth, and Robert travelled on alone.

Hours later he was met by his brother David at a little wayside station, and driven over fifteen miles of hilly road to the farm where he had been born and brought up.

Next morning he was up at daybreak, and set to work at his usual tasks about the yard, well knowing that such would be his lot to the end of his life if the examination list did not show his name at the top.

Some days had to elapse before the result could be known; but Robert Chalmers Fordyce – by the way, I think we know him well enough now to call him Robin, which was the name his mother had given him on his third birthday – and his household, being Scottish and undemonstrative, made little or no reference to the subject.

Robin was the scholar of his family. He waa the second son, David being four years older. But in accordance with that simple, grand, and

patriarchal law of Scottish peasant life, which decrees that every lad of parts shall be given his chance to bring credit on the family, even though his parents have to pinch and save and his brothers bide at the plough-tail all their lives in consequence – a law whose chief merit lies in the splendid sacrifices which its faithful fulfilment involves, and whose vital principle well - meaning but misguided philanthropy is now endeavouring to dole out of existence – he had been sent to Edinburgh to make the most of this, his one chance in life.

Still, though the credit of the family hung upon the result of the examination, – if he won the Bursary, the money, together with the precious hoard which his father and mother had been accumulating for him for ten years, would just suffice to keep him at the University, – no one discussed the matter. It was in the hands of God, and prognostication could only be vain and unprofitable. His mother and sister, indeed, questioned him covertly when his father and brother were out of hearing; but that was chiefly about Edinburgh, and the shops, and the splendours of the Dairy Road. The Bursary was never mentioned.

On the day on which the result was to beannounced their father took Robin and David away to a distant hillside to assist at the sheep- dipping. The news would come by letter, which might or might not get as far as Strathmyrtle Post Office, seven miles away, that very afternoon. In the morning it would be delivered by the postman.

But there are limits to human endurance, none the less definite because that endurance appears illimitable. When father and sons tramped back to the farm that evening, just in time for supper, it was discovered that Margaret was absent. John Fordyce, grim old martinet that he was, looked round the table inquiringly; but a glance at his wife's face caused him to go on with his meal.

At nine o'clock precisely the table was cleared. The herdman and two farm lasses came into the kitchen from their final tasks in the yard, and the great Bible was put down on the table for evening " worship."

John Fordyce, having looked up the " portion " which he proposed to read, then turned to the Metrical Psalms. These were sung night by night in unswerving rotation throughout the year, a custom which, while it offered the pleasing prospect of variety, occasionally leftsomething to be desired on the score of appropriateness.

All being seated, the old man, after a final fleeting glance at his daughter's empty chair, gave out the Psalm.

"Let us worship God," he said, "by singing to His praise in the Hundred and Twenty-first Psalm. Psalm a Hundred and Twenty-one –

' I to the hills will lift mine eyes,

From whence doth come '"

The door opened, and Margaret entered. She was dusty and tired, for she had walked fourteen miles since milking-time; but in her hand she held a letter.

She glanced timidly at the clock, and was for slipping quietly into her seat; but her father said –

"You had best give it to him now. A man cannot worship God while his mind is distracted with other things."

Robin took the letter, and after a glance in the direction of his father and the waiting Bible, opened and read it amidst a tense silence. Finally he looked up.

" Well ?" said the old man.

"They have given me the First Bursary, father," said Robin.

No one spoke, but Robin saw tears running down his mother's face. John Fordyce deliberately turned back several pages of the Bible.

" We will sing," he said in a clear voice, " in the Twenty-third Psalm – the whole of it! –

The Lord's my Shepherd, I'll not want '"

The Psalms of David, as rendered into English verse by Nahum Tate and others, are not remarkable for poetic merit; neither does the old Scottish fashion of singing the same, seated and without accompaniment, conduce to a concord of sweet sounds. But there are no tunes like old tunes, and there are no hearts like full hearts. If ever a song went straight up to heaven, the Twenty-third Psalm, borne up on the wings of "Martyrdom," did so that night.

2

SECTION 2

22

CHAPTER TWO.
INTRODUCES A PILLAR OF STATE AND THE
APPURTENANCES THEREOF.

The time had undoubtedly arrived when I must have a Private Secretary.

Kitty, for one, insisted on it. She said that I was ruining my health in the service of an ungrateful country, and added that she, personally, declined to be left a widow at twenty- eight-and-a-half to oblige anybody.

" It is exactly the wrong age," she said. " If it had happened four or five years ago, I could have done pretty well for myself. Now, I should be out of the running among the *debutantes,* and a little too young and flighty to suit a middle- aged bachelor."

I may add that my wife does not often talk in this unfeeling manner. But she suffers at times from a desire to live up to a sort of honorary reputation for sprightly humour, conferred upon her by undiscriminating admirers in the days before she became engaged to me. As a matter of fact, her solicitude on my behalf was largely due to an ambition to see a little paragraph in the newspapers, announcing that "Mr Adrian Inglethwaite, M. P., Director of the Sub-Tropical and Arctic Department at the Foreign Office, has appointed Mr Blankley Dash to be his Private Secretary."

Dolly and Dilly seconded the motion. They had not the effrontery to wrap up their motives in specious expressions of concern for my health, but stated their point of view with brutal frankness, as is their wont. I was an old dear, they conceded, and of course Kitty was Kitty; but a sister and brother - in - law were, to put it quite plainly, a hopelessly dull couple to live with: and the visits of Mesdames Dolly and Dilly to our roof-tree would, it was hinted, be more frequent and enduring if the establishment was strengthened by the addition of a presentable young man.

I consented. It was three to one. To any one acquainted with the trio of sisters arrayed against me, it will at once be apparent that " these odds " (as the halfpenny papers say) " but faintly rep- resent the superiority of the winning side."

Having thus dragged the reader without apology into the most intimate regions of my family circle, I had perhaps better introduce myself and my *entourage* a little more formally.

My name is Samuel Adrian Inglethwaite. Why I was called Samuel I do not know. Possibly my parents did. Samuel may have been a baptismal sprat set to catch a testamentary whale, but if this was so no legacy ever came my way. Personally, I am rather attached to the name, as I was called nothing else until I encountered the lady who ultimately consented to become Mrs Inglethwaite. Since that epoch in my career I have been S. Adrian Inglethwaite.

I am thirty-six years of age, and hold an appointment under Government, which, while it does not carry with it Cabinet rank – though Kitty cannot see why – is sufficiently important to make the daily papers keep my obituary notice handily pigeon-holed, in case I fall over the Thames Embankment, get run over by a motor-bus, or otherwise contravene the by-laws of the London County Council.

As no man can possibly give an unbiassed opinion of his own wife, I shall not attempt to describe mine at this juncture, except tomention that she is a woman with no fault that I can for the moment recall, beyond a predilection for belonging to societies which are better known for their aims than for their achievements, are perennially short of funds, and seem to possess no place of meeting except my drawing-room.

Dolly and Dilly are Kitty's sisters. They are twins, and their present age is, I think, nineteen. Though I say it who should not, they are both astonishingly attractive young persons, and the more I see of them the more the fact is borne in upon me. Indeed, a casual remark of mine to that effect, uttered to my wife, by an unfortunate coincidence, on the very morning upon which one of the numerous Deceased Wife's Sister's Bills passed its Second Reading in the House, gave rise to a coldness of demeanour on her part which was only dispelled by an abject apology and a dinner for two at the Savoy on mine.

To return to Dolly and Dilly. I never know them apart, and I do not think Kitty does either. Both are divinely tall and divinely fair; they are exactly like each other in form, voice, and feature; and they possess the irritating habit, not uncommon with twins, of endeavouring to exaggerate their natural resemblance by various puzzling and, I consider, unsportsmanlike devices. They wear each other's clothes indiscriminately, and are not above taking turn and turn about with the affections of unsuspecting young men, of whom they possess a considerable following. They attract admiration without effort, and, I honestly believe, without intention. Of the meaning of love they know nothing, – they are female Peter Pans, and resolutely refuse to grow up, except outwardly, – and the intrusion of that passion into their dealings with persons of the male gender is regarded by them at present as a contingency to be discouraged at all costs. The conditions under which they admit their admirers to their friendship are commendably simple and perfectly definite. If a man is adjudged by them to have attained all the complicated and inexplicable standards by which women judge the opposite sex, he is admitted into the ranks of the Good Sorts; and as such, provided that he keeps his head, has an extremely pleasant time of it. If, however, any obtuse and amorous youth persists in mistaking what Nanki-Poo once described as "customary expressions of affability" for an indication that his infatuationis reciprocated, the Twins act promptly. They have "no use" for such creatures, they once explained to me; and they proceed to rid themselves of the incubus in a fashion entirely their own.

As soon as the pressure of the *affaire* rises to danger-point – *i. e.,* when the youth begins to pay markedly more attention to one Twin than the other – he is asked, say, to lunch. Here he is made much of by the object of his affections, who looks radiant in, let us say, white *batiste;* while the unemployed Twin, in (possibly) blue poplin, holds discreetly aloof. After lunch the Twins, leaving their victim to smoke a cigar, retire swiftly to their room, where they exchange costumes, and descend again to the drawing-room. There Dolly, now arrayed in white *batiste,* enters upon the path of dalliance where Dilly left off; and Dilly, relieved from duty, crochets in a window-recess, and silently enjoys her sister's impersonation.

One of two things happens. Romeo either does not notice the difference, or else he does. If he does not, he continues to flounder heavily along in pursuit of the well-beloved, oblivious of the fact that he is wasting his efforts on an understudy. After an appropriate interval thecold truth is revealed to him in a hysterical duet, and he goes home, glaring defiantly, but feeling an entire and unmitigated ass.

Or he may actually recognise that Dilly has been replaced by Dolly, – this is what happens when the case is a really serious one, – and if this occurs he is more sorrowful than angry, poor fellow, for he sees that he is being trifled with; and your true lover is the most desperately earnest person in the world. In either case the *affaire* terminates then and there. And that is how my sisters-in-law, with adroitness and despatch, return immature and undesirable suitors to their native element. The whole proceeding reminds me irresistibly of the Undersized Fish Bill, a measure whose progress I once assisted in its course through a Committee of the House.

However, having been bidden to procure a Private Secretary, I meekly set about looking for one. One night at dinner we held a symposium on the subject, and endeavoured to evolve an outline of the kind of gentleman who was likely to suit us. The following is a *precis* of the result. I leave the intelligent reader to trace each item to its author; also the various parenthetical comments on the same : –

(a) He must be a 'Varsity man.

(b) He must be able to keep accounts, and
transact business generally.

(c) He must be content with a salary of two
hundred a-year, with board and residence in the house. (" He can have that little room off the library for a sitting-room, dear, and sleep in the old night-nursery.")

(d) He must not wear celluloid collars or

made - up ties. (" But he'll *have* to, poor dear, if the Infant Samuel only gives him two hundred a-year.")

(e) He must be prepared to run through my

speeches before I deliver them. (" I suppose that means *write* them!"), look up my subject - matter, verify my references, and so on. ("That *will* be an improvement. But what will the halfpenny papers do then, poor . things?")

(/) He must be the sort of man that one can have in to a dinner-party without any fear of accidents. ("Yes. He *must* be all right about peas, asparagus, and liqueurs. *And* finger - bowls, dearest. You remember the man who drank outof his at that queer political dinner to the constituents ? ")

(g) He must be nice to my Philly.

(h) He must be dark. ("Pshaw!")

(i) He must be fair. (" Ugh !")

(j) He must be able to waltz and play bridge.

At this point I suggested that a prepaid telegram to the Celestial Regions would alone procure the article we required. However, we ultimately descended to an advertisement in the *Morning Post,* and in due course I obtained a secretary. In fact, I obtained several. We had them *seriatim,* and none stayed longer than a month. I do not propose to write a detailed history of the dynasty which I now found it my privilege to support. A brief *resume* of each will suffice.

Number One. – Cambridge Football Blue. Big and breezy. Spelling entirely phonetic. Spent most of his time smoking in the drawing-room, and laboured under the delusion that, as my amanuensis, he was at liberty to forge my signature to all documents, including cheques. He used my official note-paper to back horses on, and was finally requested to leave, after an unseemly brawl with a book-maker's tout on my doorstep.

Number Two. – Oxford: a First in Greats. A heavy manner, usually beginning his observations with "Wherewithal" or "Peradventure." The Twins suffered severely from suppressed giggles in his presence. Regarded my superficial ideas of statesmanship with profound contempt, but left after a fortnight, having allowed a highly confidential and extremely personal pencil note, written in the margin of a despatch by the Premier himself, to blossom forth in large type in the text of a Blue Book.

Number Three. – Rather elderly for the post – nearer forty than thirty – but highly recommended. Reduced my chaotic papers to order in twenty-four hours, charmed my wife and her sisters, drafted a speech which won me quite a little ovation in the House, suggested several notable improvements in the " Importation of Mad Dogs Bill," with which I was to be entrusted next session – and was found lying dead drunk in his bedroom, at eleven o'clock in the morning, on the second Sunday after his arrival. Half a dozen empty brandy bottles were afterwards discovered on the top of his wardrobe. Poor devil!

Number Four. – (Subsequently handed down to posterity as " The Limit"). Small, spectacled, and nervous. Came from a Welsh University, and was strong on "the methodical filing of State and other documents." He stayed two days. On the first night (after inquiring whether we were expecting guests that evening, and receiving an answer in the negative) he came down to dinner in a sort of alpaca smoking-jacket and a tartan tie. On the second, having evidently decided to treat us to all the resources of his wardrobe as soon as possible, he appeared in more or less ordinary evening attire. He wore a small white satin bow-tie, attached to his collar-stud by a brass clip. The tie fell off the stud into his soup almost immediately, and its owner, after furtively chasing it round the plate with his forefinger, finally fished it out with the aid of a fork; and, having squeezed as much soup as possible back into the plate, put the bow into his waistcoat pocket and resumed his meal with every appearance of enjoyment.

He left next morning. As the Twins pathetically observed : "It had to be him or us!" I was sorry, for he was a tidy little creature away from table.

After that I did a rash thing. I engaged a Private Secretary on the spur of the moment and without consulting my household.

One morning I had occasion to visit the British Museum. That mausoleum of learning is not an habitual resort of mine, but on this occasion I had found it necessary to refresh my memory on the subject of a small principality situated somewhere in the Pacific, and reported to be in a state of considerable unrest, concerning which the member for Upper Gumbtree, an unpleasantly omniscient young man with a truculent manner, had been asking questions in the House. It seemed that British interests in that quarter were not being adequately protected by our Department, and this extremely pushing gentleman was now gaining much cheap applause in the columns of those low-priced organs which make a living by deriding his Majesty's Ministers, by bombarding us with fatuous inquiries on the subject. My Chief had only the most hazy notion about the place – as a matter of fact I do not believe that either he or any of the permanent officials had ever heard of it – and I was in a precisely similar condition. I was accordingly bidden to get up the subject, and accumulate a mass of information thereon which would not only satiate the appetite of the honourable member, but choke him off for all time.

Finding myself in want of a particular Gazetteer which was not to be found in the office, and being in no mood to take a clerk, however uncritical, into my confidence, I called a hansom and drove straight to the Museum; where, having ensconced myself in the reading- room with the work in question, I prepared to devote a dusty and laborious morning to the service of State.

Immediately opposite me sat a gigantic young man of a slightly threadbare appearance, who was copying some screed out of a bulky tome before him. I regarded him in a reminiscent sort of way for a few minutes, and presently found that my scrutiny was being returned fourfold. Next came an enormous hand that was suddenly thrust across the table towards me, and I remembered him.

We had met six years ago in a railway train, under circumstances which made me extremely glad to make his acquaintance at any price. Kitty and I were on our honeymoon, and happened to be travelling on a Saturday afternoon from Edinburgh to Perth in a train packed to suffocation with the supporters of a football team of the baser sort. We were bound for Inchellan, the Scottish residence of my Chief, who was sending to meet us at Perth.

As the first-class carriages were all occupied by gentlemen with third-class tickets, we travelled third with a company who did not seem to possess any tickets at all. Just before the train started the door was thrown open and two inebriated Scots, several degrees further gone than the rest of the company – which is saying a goodvdeal – were hurled in. If the assemblage had all been of one way of thinking we might have reached Perth with nothing worse than bad headaches, but unfortunately some supporters of the other team were present and in the midst of a heated and alcoholic debate on the rights and wrongs of the last free kick, two rival orators suddenly arose, clinched, and continued their argument at close grips on the floor. In a moment the party divided itself into two camps, and the conflict became general. As there were ten people in the compartment, of whom seven were engaged in a life-and-death struggle, the movements of the non - combatants – Kitty, myself, and a gigantic youth of gawky appearance – were, to put it mildly, somewhat restricted. Kitty became thoroughly frightened, and hampered my preparations for battle by clinging to my arm. The gigantic youth, seeing this, suddenly took command of the situation.

" Watch you the young leddy! he bellowed in my ear, "and I'll sort them."

With that he hurled himself into the tumult. The exact details of his performance I could not see, the scientific dusting of railway cushions not having penetrated any further north of the Forth than it has south of the Thames; but the net result was that each combatant was pulled *off,* picked up, shaken until his teeth rattled, and banged down on to his seat with a brief admonition to mind his manners, until seven bewildered, partially sobered, and thoroughly demoralised patrons of sport sat round about in various attitudes of limp dejection, leaning against one another like dissipated marionettes; while our rustic Hector, bestriding the compartment like a Colossus, dared them to move a finger under penalty of being "skelped."

He bundled them all out at the next stopping- place, without inquiring whether they desired to alight there or no, and I am bound to say that they all seemed as anxious to leave the carriage as he was to expel them. He then shut the door, pulled up the window, and turned to my wife with a reassuring smile.

"Yon was just a storrm in a teapot," he remarked affably.

He accepted my thanks with indifference, but blushed in a gratified manner when Kitty addressed him. He was her bond-slave by the time that we bade him farewell at Perth. I presented him with my card, which he carefully placed inside the lining of his hat; but he forbore, either from native caution or excessive shyness, to furnish us with any information as to his own identity.

Well, here he was, sitting opposite to me in the Beading Boom of the British Museum, and seemingly none too prosperous. Six years ago he had looked like a young and healthy farm lad. Now, fourth-rate journalism was stamped all over him.

CHAPTER THREE.

" ANENT."

We conversed awhile in whispers to avoid disturbing the other worshippers – I always feel like that in the British Museum – and finally abandoned our respective tasks and issued forth together. With a little persuasion I prevailed upon my companion to come and lunch with me, and we repaired to a rather old-fashioned and thoroughly British establishment close by, where the fare is solid and the " portions " generous.

My guest, after a brief effort at self-repression, fell upon the food in a fashion that told me a far more vivid tale of his present circumstances than the most lengthy explanation could have done. When he was full I gave him a cigar, and he leaned back in his padded arm-chair and surveyed me with the nearest approach to emotion that I have ever observed in the countenance of a Scot.

" I was wanting that," he remarked frankly, and he smiled largely upon me. He was looking less gaunt now, and the rugged lines of his face were tinged with a more healthy colour. He was a handsome youth, I noticed, with shrewd grey eyes and a chin that stood out like the ram of a battle-ship.

He told me all about himself, some of which has been set down here already. He had done well at Edinburgh University, and, having obtained his Arts degree, was on the point of settling down to study for the ministry – the be-all and end-all of the hope of a humble Scottish household – when disaster came tumbling upon his family. His brother David fell sick in his lungs, and the doctor prescribed a sojourn in a drier climate for at least a year.

The next part of the narrative was rather elliptical; but from the fact that money was immediately forthcoming to send David abroad, and that Robin had simultaneously given up his work in Edinburgh and returned home to help his father about the farm, I gathered that a life's ambition had been voluntarily sacrificed on the altar of family duty. Anyhow, when David returned, marvellously and mercifullyrestored to health, setting his younger brother free once more, two precious years had flown; so that Robin now found himself, at the age of twenty-three, faced with the alternative of making a fresh start in life or remaining on the farm at home, that most pathetic and forlorn of failures, a " stickit minister." The family exchequer had been depleted by David's illness, and Robin, rather than draw any further on the vanishing little store of pound-notes in the cupboard behind the kitchen chimney, determined to go to London and turn his education to some account.

He had arrived three years ago, with a barrel of salt herrings and a bag of meal; and from that time he had earned his own living – if it could be called a living.

"Once or twice," he said, "I have had an article taken by one of the big reviews; sometimes I get some odd reporting to do; and whiles I just have to -write chatty paragraphs about celebrities for the snippety papers."

"Uphill work that, I should think."

" Uphill ? Downhill! Man, it's degrading. Do you know what I was doing in that Museum this morning?"

"What?"

"Have you heard tell of a man they call Dean Ramsay?"

" Let me see – yes. He was a sort of Scottish Sidney Smith, wasn't he ? "

"That is the man. Well, he collected most of the good stories in Scotland and put them in a book. I was copying a few of them out; and I shall father them on to folk that the public wants to hear about. I get a guinea a column for that."

"I know the sort of thing," I said. *"A good story is at present going the round of the clubs, concerning* "

" Not ' concerning' – ' anent'!"

" I beg your pardon – ' anent a certain well-known but absent - minded Peer of the Realm.'"

"That's the stuff You have the trick of it. Then sometimes I do bits of general information – computations as to the height of a column of the picture postcards sold in London in a year, and all that. Nobody can check figures of that kind, so the work is easy – and correspondingly ill-paid!" (I cannot reproduce the number of contemptuous *r'&* that Robin threw into the adverb.)

"It's a fine useful place the Museum," hecontinued reflectively. "You were busy there this morning yourself You would be collecting *data* anent – I mean *about* – the Island of Caerulea."

I sat up in surprise at this.

" How on earth ? " I began.

" Oh, I just jal – guessed it. You being the only member of his Majesty's Government in whom I have any personal interest, -I have always followed your career closely. (You gave me your card, you'll mind.) Well, I saw you were having trouble with yon havering body Wuddiford – I once reported at one of his meetings : he's just a sweetie-wife in *pince-nez* – and when I saw you busy with an atlas and gazetteer I said to myself: – 'He'll be getting up a few salient facts about the place, in order to appease the honourable member's insatiable thirst for knowledge – Toots, there I go again! Man, the journalese fairly soaks into the system. I doubt now if I could write out twenty lines of ' Paradise Lost' without cross - heading them!"

We finished our cigar over talk like this, and finally rose to go. Robin lingered upon the steps of the restaurant. I realised that he, being a Scotsman, was endeavouring to pumpup the emotional gratitude which he felt sure that I, as an Englishman, would expect from a starving pauper who had lunched at my expense.

" I must thank you," he said at last, [rather awkwardly, " for a most pleasant luncheon. And I should like fine," he added suddenly and impetuously, " to make out a *precis* for you on the subject of Caerulea. Never heed it yourself! Away home, and I'll send it to you to-morrow!"

An idea which had been maturing in my slow-moving brain for some time suddenly took a definite shape.

"It is extremely kind of you," I said. "I shall be delighted to leave the matter in your hands. But when you have made the *precis,* I wonder if you would be so good as to bring it to my house instead of sending it ? "

I gave him my address, and we parted.

Robert Chalmers Fordyce arrived at my house next morning. He brought with him a budget of condensed but exhaustive information on the subject of Caerulea, the assimilation and ultimate discharge of which enabled me to score a signal victory over Mr Wuddiford of Upper Gumbtree, relegating that champion exploiter of mare's neststo a sphere of comparative inoffensiveness for quite a considerable time.

After reading the *precis, I* oifered Robin the position of my Private Secretary, which he accepted politely but without servility or effusiveness. I handed him a quarter's salary in advance, gave him two days' holiday wherein to " make his arrangements" – *Anglic,* to replenish his wardrobe – and we sealed the bargain with a glass of sherry and a biscuit apiece.

As he rose to go, Robin took from his pocket a folded manuscript.

" I see you have a good fire there," he said.

He stepped across to the hearth-rug and pitched the document into the heart of the flames, which began to lick it caressingly.

Presently the heat caused the crackling paper to unfold itself, and some of the writing became visible. Robert pointed, and I read –

"Pars about Personalities. A capital story is at present going the round of the clubs, anent "

Here the flimsy manuscript burst into flame, and shot with a roar up the chimney.

I looked at Robert Chalmers Fordyce, and his face was the face of a man who has gonethrough deep waters, but feels the good solid rock beneath his feet at last.

He turned dumbly to me, and held out his hand.

The worst of these inarticulate and undemonstrative people is that they hurt you so.

CHAPTER FOUP

A TRIAL TRIP.

Three days later I introduced Robert Chalmers Fordyce into the bosom of my family. I had declined to give them any previous information about him, beyond a brief warning that they would find him "rather Scotch."

I have always found it utterly impossible to foretell from a man's behaviour towards his own sex how he will comport himself in the presence of females. I have known a raw youth, hitherto regarded as the hobbledehoy of the shooting-party and the pariah of the smoking-room, lord it among the ladies like a very lion; and I have seen the hero of a hundred fights, the master of men, the essence of intrepid resolution, stand quaking outside a drawing-room door. The *ddbut* of Piobin, then, I awaited with considerable interest. I expected on the whole to see him tongue-tied, especiallybefore Dolly and Dilly. On the other hand he might be aggressively assertive.

He was neither. He proved to be that ' rarest of types – the man who has no fear of his fellow-creatures, male or female, singly or in battalions. Our sex is so accustomed to squaring its shoulders, pulling down its waistcoat, and assuming an engaging expression as a preliminary to an encounter with the fair, that the spectacle of a man who enters a strange drawing-room and shakes hands quietly and naturally all round, without twisting his features into an agreeable smile and mumbling entirely inarticulate words of rapture, always arouses in me feelings of envy and respect.

We found Kitty and the Twins picturesquely grouped upon the drawing-room hearth-rug, waiting for the luncheon gong.

I introduced Robin to my wife, in the indistinct and throaty tones which always obtrude themselves into an Englishman's utterance when he is called upon to say something formal but graceful. Kitty greeted the guest with a smile with which I am well acquainted (and which I can guarantee from personal experience to be absolutely irresistible on one's first experience of it), and welcomed him to the house very prettily.

"You are very kind, Mrs Inglethwaite," said Robin, shaking hands. "But I am not quite a stranger to you. Do you mind my face?"

Kitty turned scarlet.

" Mind your ? Not in the – I mean – I am
sure we are de " She floundered hopelessly.

Robin laughed pleasantly.

"There is my Scots tongue running away with me already," he said. " I should have asked rather if you *remembered* my face."

This time Kitty ceased to look confused, but still retained a puzzled frown.

"No," she said slowly; "I don't *think* "

" No wonder!" said Robin. " We met once, in a railway carriage, six years ago. Between Edinburgh and Perth – on a Saturday afternoon," he added expressively.

Light broke in upon Kitty. "Of course!" she said. " Now I remember. That dreadful journey! You were the gentleman who was so kind and helpful. How nice and romantic meeting again! Adrian, you silly old creature, why didn't you tell me? Now, Mr Fordyce, let me introduce you to my sisters."

She wheeled him round and presented him to the Twins.

That pair of beauties, I saw at a glance, were out after scalps. They stood up side by side on the hearth-rug, absolutely and weirdly alike, and arrayed on this occasion in garments of identical hue and cut. This was a favourite device [of theirs when about to meet a new young man; it usually startled him considerably. If he was not a person of sound nerve and abstemious habits, it not infrequently evoked from him some enjoyably regrettable expression of surprise and alarm. I knew all the tricks in their *repertoire,* and waited interestedly to see the effect of this series.

On being presented, both smiled shyly and modestly, and each simultaneously proffered a timid hand. The average young man, already a little rattled by the duplicate vision of loveliness before him, could never make up his mind which hand to shake first; and by the time he had collected his faculties sufficiently to make an uncertain grab at one, both would be swiftly and simultaneously withdrawn.

Robin, however, immediately shook hands with Dilly, who stood nearest to Kitty, and then with Dolly. After that he stepped back a pace and surveyed the pair with unconcealed interest.

Then he turned to my wife.

"A truly remarkable resemblance!" he observed benignantly. ("Just as if we had been two babies in a bassinette!" as Dolly afterwards remarked.)

Then he resumed his inspection. The Twins, who were entirely unused to this sort of thing, were too taken aback to proceed to their second move – the utterance of some trivial and artless remark, delivered by both simultaneously, and thereby calculated to throw the victim into a state of uncertainty as to which he should answer first. Instead, they stood wide-eyed and tongue-tied before him.

"I must certainly discover some point of difference between these ladies," continued Robin with an air of determination, "or I shall always be in difficulties. Do not tell me the secret, Mrs Inglethwaite. Perhaps I can find out for myself."

He concluded a minute inspection of the indignant Dilly, and turned his unruffled gaze on Dolly.

"Yes," he said, "I have it! You" (triumphantly to Dolly) "have a tiny brown spot in the blue of your left eye, while your sister has none."

It was quite true: she had. But it was a fact which most young men "only discovered after many furtive and sidelong glances. This imperturbable creature had taken it all in in one resolute scrutiny; and Dolly, blushing like Aurora – an infirmity to which I may say neither she nor her sister are particularly subject – dropped her long lashes over the orbs in question and looked uncommonly foolish.

The tension of the situation was relieved by the announcement of luncheon, and Robin was called upon to accompany Kitty downstairs; while I, putting a consoling arm round the waist of each of my fermenting sisters-in-law, marched them down to further experiences in the dining-room.

The Twins rapidly recovered their equanimity at lunch. They sat, as they always did, together on one side of the table, opposite to Robin. The latter conversed easily and pleasantly, though his discourse was dotted with homely phrases and curious little biblical turns of speech.

"Have you been in London long, Mr For- dyce?" inquired Kitty as we settled down.

"Three years," said Robin.

"I suppose you have lots of friends by this time."

"I have a good many acquaintances, but my friends in London are just three, all told," said Robin, in what Dilly afterwards described as "a disgustingly pawky manner."

"You must be very exclusive, Mr Fordyce," chirrupped Dolly.

" Far from it," said Robin ; " as you will admit when I say that my three friends are a policeman, a surgeon, and a minister."

" How quaint of you!" said Dilly.

But Robin did not seem to think it quaint. He told us about the policeman first – a Highlander. Robin had made his acquaintance in Edinburgh, apparently about the same time that he made ours, and had renewed it some years later outside the House of Commons, when a rapturous mutual recognition had taken place. The policeman's name was Hector MacPherson.

"And the surgeon?" inquired Kitty, with a certain friendly assumption of interest which announces (to me) that she is getting a little bored.

"He is just my uncle. I go and see him, whi – now and then. He is a busy man."

" And the – er – minister ? "

" He is Dr Strang. He has the PresbyterianChurch in Howard Street. I have sat under him every Sabbath since I came to London."

."Wh – what for?" asked Kitty involuntarily, and in a rather awestruck voice. Her acquaintance with the ritual of the Church of Scotland was hazy, and she was evidently determined to-day to be surprised at nothing; but evidently this mysterious reference could not be allowed to pass without some explanation. The Twins convulsively gripped each other's hands under the table. (They are of course perfectly bred girls – indeed, their self- possession at trying moments has often surprised me – but, like all the young of the human species, there are times when their feelings become too much for them. Then, if the occasion is too formal for unrestrained shrieks, they silently interdigitate.)

"That is a Scottish expression," said Robin, smiling upon us. " You must pardon me, Mrs Inglethwaite. I should perhaps have said that I was an *adherent* of Dr Strang's church – or rather," he added with a curious little touch of pride, "I am a communicant now. I was just an adherent at first."

We assented to this, politely but dizzily.

Scratch a Scot and you will find a theologian.

Robin was fairly started now; and he proceeded to enlarge upon various points of interest in the parallel histories (given in full) of some three or four Scottish denominations, interwoven with extracts from his own family archives. His grand-uncle, it appeared, had been a minister himself, and had performed the feat – to which I have occasionally heard other perfervid Scots refer, and never without a kindling eye – known as "coming out in the Forty-three."

"That," added Robin in parenthesis, "is why my second name is Chalmers – after the great Doctor. You will have heard of him ?"

(Polite but insincere chorus of pleased recognition.)

We were then treated to a brief *rdsumd* of the events leading up to a religious controversy of colossal dimensions which was at that moment threatening to engulf Scotland. Robin was deeply interested in the matter, and gave us his reasons for being so. He passed some scathing comments on the contumacy and narrow-mindedness of the sect who had the misfortune to be his opponents; and after that he proceeded to say a few words about Free Will and Predestination.

By this time lunch was over, but we saton. I nodded gravely over my coffee, saying " Quite so" when occasion seemed to demand it. Kitty was completely out of her depth, but still maintained a brave appearance of interest. It was the Twins who brought the *stance* to a close. Placing their hands before their mouths, they with difficulty stifled a pair of cavernous yawns.

Next moment they were sorry. Robin stopped dead, flushed up, and said –

"Mrs Inglethwaite, I am sorry. I have been most inconsiderate and rude. I have wearied you all. The truth is," he continued quite simply, "it is so long since I sat at meat with friends, that I have lost the art of conversation. I just run on, like – like a leading article. I have not conversed with a woman, except once or twice across a counter, for nearly three years."

There was a rather tense pause. Then Dolly said –

"We're awfully sorry, Mr Fordyce. It was very rude of us. We quite understand now, don't we, Dilly?"

"Bather," said Duly. "It was horrible of us, Mr Fordyce. But we thought you were just an ordinary bore."

"Children!" said Kitty.

"But what you have told us makes things quite different, doesn't it, Dolly?" continued Dilly.

" Quite – absolutely," said Dolly,

And they smiled upon him, quite maternally. And so the incident passed.

"How queer, not talking to a woman for three years!" continued Dolly reflectively.

"How *awful* it would be not to talk to a man for three years!" said Dilly, with obvious sincerity.

" There is little opportunity for social intercourse," said Robin, "to a man who comes to London to sink or swim."

The conversation was again taking a slightly sombre turn, and I struck in –

" Well, I hope, Mr Fordyce, that a few weeks' experience of my establishment won't have the effect of making you regret your previous celibate existence."

Dolly and Dilly looked at each other.

" Dolly," said Dilly, " is that an insult ? "

" I think so."

" Insulting enough to be punishable ? "

"Bather."

"All right. Come on 1"

They fell upon me, and the next few minutes were devoted to what I believe is known in pantomime circles as a Grand Rally, which necessitated my going upstairs afterwards and changing my collar.

Robin was not present at tea, and my household took advantage of his absence to run over his points.

Considering that a woman – especially a young woman – judges a man almost entirely by his manner and appearance, and dislikes him exceedingly if he proceeds to dominate the situation to her exclusion – unless, by the way, he has her permission and authority so to do, in which case he cannot do so too much – the verdict delivered upon my absent secretary was not by any means unfavourable, though, of course, there was much to criticise.

"He'll do," said Duly; "but you must get his hair cut, Adrian."

"And tell him about not wearing that sort of tie, dear," said Dolly.

"I suppose he can't help his accent," sighs

But their criticisms were limited to such trifles as these, and I felt that Robin had done me credit.

Dilly summed up the situation.

"I think on the whole that he is rather a pet," she said.

A more thoroughly unsuitable description could not have been imagined, but Dolly agreed.

" He has nice eyes, too," she added.

"He was perfectly sweet with Phillis after lunch," said Kitty. "Took her on his knee at once, and talked to her just as if we weren't there. That's a good test of a man, if you like!"

"True for you," I agreed. "I could not do it with other people's children to save my life."

"Oh, you are hopeless," said Dilly. "*Fcur* too self-conscious and dignified to climb down to the level of children, isn't he, Dolly ?" She crinkled her nose.

Dolly for once was not listening.

"What was that weird stuff the Secretary Bird spouted when you showed Phillis to him, Kit ? About her being forward, or coy, or something. It sounded rather cheek, to me."

"Yes, I remember," said Dilly. "Can you do the way he said it ? ' Sometimes forrrwarrrd, sometimes coy, she neverrr fails to pullllease!' Like thatl Gracious, how it hurts to talk Scotch!"

"I don't know, dear," said my wife thoughtfully. "It Bounded rather quaint. But I daresay all Scotch people are like that," she added charitably.

" Perhaps it was a quotation," I observed mildly.

" Of course, that would be it. What is it out of?"

"A song called 'Phillis is my only Joy,' I think."

"Ah, then you may depend upon it," said Kitty, with the air of one solving a mystery, "that is what the man was doing – *quoting!* Burns," probably, or Scott, perhaps. How clever of him to think of it 1 And do you know," she continued, "he said such a nice thing to me. While you were bear-fighting with the Twins after lunch, Adrian, I *[said* to him: ' Pity me, Mr Fordyce! My husband never ceases to express to me his regret that he did not marry one of my sisters.' And he answered at once, quite seriously, without stopping to think it out or anything: – 'I am surg, Mrs Inglethwaite, that his regret must be shared by countless old admirers of yours!' Wasn't it rather sweet of him ?"

Further conversation was prevented by theopening of the drawing-room door, where the butler appeared and announced "Mr Dubberley."

Dubberley is a pillar of our party. I can best describe him by saying that although I hold office under a Conservative Government, ten minutes' conversation with Dubberley leaves me a confirmed Radical, and anything like a protracted interview with him converts me into a Socialist for the next twenty-four hours. A week-end in his society, and I should probably buy a red shirt and send out for bombs. He is a good fellow at bottom, and of immense service to the party; but he is the most blatant ass I have ever met. There are Dubberleya on both sides of the House, however, which is a comfort.

Robin joined us almost directly after Dubber- ley's entrance, just in time to hear that great man conclude the preamble of his discourse for the afternoon.

There had been a good deal of talk in the papers of late about improving the means of transport throughout the country; and the nationalisation of railways and other semi - socialistic schemes had filled the air. Dubberley, it appeared, had out of his own giganticintellect evolved a panacea for congestion of traffic, highness of rates, and railway mortality.

He was well launched in his subject when Robin entered and was introduced.

"As I was saying," he continued, waving an emphatic teaspoon in the direction of the sofa where the ladies sat, smiling but limp, – even the Twins knew it was useless to stem this tide, – "as I was saying, the solution of the problem lies in the revival of our far-reaching but sadly neglected system of *canals.* Yes! If we go to the very root of the matter" – Dub- berley is one of those fortunate persons who never has to dig far in his researches – " we find that our whole hope of regeneration lies ia the single, simple, homely word – Canals! Revive your canals, send your goods by canal, travel yourself by "

" How long, Mr Dubberley," interpolated Robin, leaning forward – "how long do you consider one would take to travel, say, a hundred miles by canal?"

" Under our present antiquated system, sir," – Dubberley rather prides himself on preserving the courtly fashions of address of a bygone age, – " an impossibly long time. The average speed of a canal-boat at the present day under theministrations of that overburdened and inadequate quadruped, the – er – horse, is three miles per hour. Indeed – one moment!"

Dubberley fished a sheaf of documents out of his pocket – he is the sort of man who habitually secrets statistics and blue-books about his person – and after stertorously perusing them closed his eyes for a moment, as if to work out a sum upon an internal blackboard, and said –

" I see no reason why swift canal - boats should not be constructed to run fifteen, twenty, or even twenty-five miles per hour. Indeed, in these days of turbines "

Robin put down his cup rather emphatically, and said –

" Mphm."

(It is quite impossible to reproduce this extraordinary Caledonian expletive in writing, but that is as near to it as I can get.) Then he continued urbanely –

"Then you would organise a service of fast turbine steamers running all over the canal systems of the country ? "

" Exactly. Or let us say – er – launches," said Dubberley. "I must not overstate my case."

" Travelling twenty miles an hour ?"

"Say fifteen, sir," said Dubberley magnanimously.

" Mr Dubberley," said Kobin, in a voice which made us all jump, "have you a bathroom in your house?"

Even the Twins, who were growing a trifle lethargic under the technicalities of the subject, roused themselves at this fresh turn of the conversation.

" Ah – eh – I beg your pardon ? " said Dubberley, a trifle disconcerted.

" A bathroom," repeated Robin – "with a good long bath in it ? "

"Er – yes."

" Well, Mr Dubberley, when you go home this afternoon, go upstairs and fill the bath with water. Then take a large bath-sponge – something nearly as broad as the bath – and sweep it along from end to end, about a foot below the surface, at a speed of fifteen miles per hour – that will be twenty-two feet per second – and see what happens!"

Robin had unconsciously dropped into what I may call his debating-society manner. His chin stuck out, and his large chest heaved, and he scooped the air, as if it had been the water of Dubberley's bath, with one of Kitty's priceless Worcester teacups.

Dubberley sat completely demoralised, palpitating like a stranded frog.

" Then," continued Robin, " you would observe the result of placing a partly submerged and rapidly moving body in a shallow and restricted waterway. You would kick half the water right out of the canal to begin with, and the other half would pile itself up into a wave under your bow big enough to offer an almost immovable resistance to the progress of your vessel."

He leaned back and surveyed the bemused Dubberley with complete and obvious satisfaction. We all sat round breathless, feeling much as Sidney Smith must have felt when some one spoke disrespectfully of the Equator. Great was the fall of Dubberley. He moved, perhaps instinctively, in a society where he was seldom contradicted and never argued with. One does not argue with a gramophone. And here this raw Scottish youth, with the awful thoroughness and relentless common-sense of his race, had taken the very words out of his mouth, torn them to shreds, and thrust them down his throat.

I am afraid I chuckled. The Twins sat hand in hand, with dreamy eyes staring straight beforethem. They were conjuring up a joyous vision of Dubberley, in his shirt

- sleeves, meekly refuting one of his own theories by means of a childish and sloppy experiment in practical hydrodynamics in his own bathroom.

I give this incident as a fair example of Robin's point of view and methods of action on questions which I for one would never dream of debating. He was entirely lacking in an art which I am told I possess to perfection – that of suffering fools gladly. Its possession has raised me to an Under - Secretaryship. People who should know tell me that it will also prevent my ever rising to anything higher.

"We had a taste of our friend's quality this afternoon," I remarked to my household when we met for dinner that evening. " He is a thorough-going warrior. Fancy any man taking all that trouble to lay out old Dubberley!"

"Poor Mr Dubberley 1" said tender-hearted Kitty.

" Do him good!" said Dilly, in Twhose recollection Dubberley's past enormities loomed large. "I shall be nice to the Secretary Bird now."

Dolly said nothing, which was unusual. Perhaps the brown spot still rankled.

CHAPTER FIVE.

ROBIN ON DUTY.

Beyond the fact that they are all desperately in earnest, all know each other, and occupy all the most responsible and lucrative posts on the face of the earth, Scotsmen are a class with whose characteristics I am not well acquainted. But I learned a great deal from my new secretary.

Robin soon settled down to work. He not only performed his duties with zeal and discretion, but he kept me up to mine. He hounded me through the routine work of my Department; he verified my references; he managed my correspondence; and he frequently drafted my speeches. He even prepared some of my impromptus. Indeed, my – or rather his – description of a certain member of the other side, a lesser light of the last Government, a worthy man, always put up to explain matterswhen his leader had decided that honesty on this occasion was the best policy, as " a political niblick, always employed to get his party out of bad lies," won me more applause and popularity in a House of enthusiastic golfers than endless weeks of honest toil behind the scenes had ever done.

But I learned more from "Robin than that. I suppose I am a typical specimen of Conservative officialdom. Until Robin came into my house it had never occurred to me to ask myself why I was a Conservative: I had been born one, and it was difficult for me to understand how any man of ordinary intelligence could be anything

My father and grandfather were Conservative members before me, and I come of a line which has always feared God, honoured the King, paid its tithes, and tried to do something for the poor; and which regards Radicals, Socialists, Nonconformists, and criminal lunatics as much the same class of person. The only difference between myself and my forebears is that I am much too pacific (or lazy) to cherish any animosity against people whose views differ from my own. This fact, coupled with certain family traditions, has brought me to my presentposition in life; and, as I have already indicated, it will probably keep me there. At least, so Kitty says.

" You must *assert* yourself, dear," she declares. "Be *rude* to people, and go on being rude! Then they will take notice of you and give you nice big posts to keep you quiet. Do you know what the Premier said about you the other night at dinner, to

Lady Bindle ? (She told Dicky Lever, and he told the Twins.) Inglethwaite ? A dear fellow, a sound party man, and runs his Department admirably. But – he strikes only on the box !' Pig !"

It was about this time that Robin became a member of our establishment. I had no idea what his political views were – it was just like me not to have asked him, Kitty said – but felt confident that whatever side he supported he would do so hot and strong.

But at first he gave no indication of his leanings. It was not until we sat one night over our wine, in company with John Champion (member for a big northern constituency, and regarded by many, notwithstanding various eccentricities, as the coming man of the party) that he first gave definite utterance to his views.

The cigars had gone round, and we had just performed that mysterious national rite which, whether it owes its existence to economy or politeness, invariably ends in several people burning their fingers with the same match.

" I suppose, Mr Fordyce," said Champion, who had not met Robin before, but obviously liked him, " that in common with all Scotsmen you are at heart a Radical."

" Am I ? " said Robin, with native caution.

"Most of your countrymen are," said Champion, with a sigh. " ' They think too much' – you know the rest of the quotation, I expect."

Robin nodded.

I was a little scandalised at this flagrant tribute to the enemy, and said so.

Champion laughed.

" You are a whole - hearted old war - horse, Adrian. I envy you. Sometimes, I wish that I "

"For mercy's sake don't go and say that you are a Radical at heart too," I cried.

"N-n-o. But isn't it rot, the whole business ?"

"What whole business?"

"Ask Mr Fordyce there. He will tell you. *I* see it in his eye."

"What is rot, Robin?" I asked. "Party government ?"

"Yes," said Robin, quite explosively for him. "It is such a scandalous waste of power and material." He laid down his cigar. " Man, it's just pitiful. Consider! A party is returned to office. With great care and discrimination a Cabinet is chosen. It is composed of men who are mainly honest and patriotic. They are not necessarily men of genius, but they are all men of undoubted ability, and they are genuinely anxious to do their duty by the country. Now observe." (As a matter of fact he said " obsairrve.") " How is this energy and ability expended? About half of it – fifty per cent' – goes in devising means to baffle the assaults of the Opposition and so retain a precarious hold on office. Sir, it's just ludicrous! Instead of concentrating their efforts upon – upon – I want a metaphor, Mr Champion."

" Upon steering the ship of State," said Champion, with a twinkle in his eye.

"That'll do, fine. – Upon steering the ship of State, they have to devote half their time and energy to dodging the missiles of their shipmates. That is what I mean when I say the thing is pitifuL What should we think of the sanity of an ordinary ship's company, if the man at the wheel had to spend half his time up in the rigging because a minority of his messmates wanted to throw him overboard ? "

" I think you are putting the case too strongly," I said. "The criticism of a healthy public opinion is no bad thing. Besides, your Cabinet still have fifty per cent of their energy left. What do they do with that?"

" Of that," said Champion, joining in, " about forty per cent is wasted on mere parade – dummy legislation – bills that never will be passed, and which no sensible man has any desire should be passed, except in a mutilated and useless condition; bills merely brought forward by the Government as a sop to the extreme wing of their own party. It doesn't matter which side is in power. If they are Liberals, they have to propose a few socialistic and iconoclastic measures, secretly thanking God for the House of Lords all the while. If they are Conservatives, they propitiate the Landlords and the Church by putting forward some outrageously retrograde proposal or other, secure in the knowledge that it will be knocked on the head by the halfpenny papers. Of the remaining ten per cent "

"About nine," resumed Robin, "is appropriated automatically to absolutely essential routine business, like the Budget and Supply "

"And the remaining one per cent," struck in Champion, "is devoted to real live Legislation."

Then they both looked at me, this pair of carping pessimists, rather furtively, like two fags who have allowed their tongues to wag over freely in the presence of a monitor. It was a curious tribute to the power of officialdom, for they were both far bigger men, in every sense, than I. Finally Champion laughed.

"Don't look so horrified, Adrian," he said. " Mr Fordyce and I croak too much. Still, you will find a grain or two of sense among the chaff, as Jack Point says."

But I was not to be smoothed down so easily.

"According to you fellows," I grumbled, as I passed the port, "there is practically no difference between one political party and another "

" None whatever," said Champion cheerfully – " not between the *backbones* of the parties, that is. Of course excrescences don't count. Tell me, Adrian, what bill, barring one or two contentious semi-religious measures, has ultimately reached the Statute Book during the last twenty yearsthat might not have been put there by either party without any violent departure from its principles ? Not one! Foreign policy, again. Does it make any difference to our position in the world *which* party is in office nowadays? Not a scrap. The difference between the two sides is immaterial. There is often a far deeper line of cleavage between two sections of the same party than between party and party. We make faces at each other, it is true; and one side plumes itself on the moral support of Royalty and the aristocracy, while the other always bawls out that it has the inviolable will of the people at its back, – I daresay one assertion is about as true as the other – but I don't think there is a pennyworth of difference, really. There *used* to be a lot, mind you, when the Plebs were really struggling for a footing in the scheme of things; but bless you! we are all more or less in the same crowd now. Just a difference of label, that's all."

" There was a story my dominie used to tell," said Robin, who had been listening to this diatribe with rapt attention, "about a visitor to a seaside hotel, who ordered a bottle of wine. The boy brought up the wrong kind, so the visitor sent for the landlord and pointed out themistake, adducing the label on the bottle as evidence. ' I'm very sorry, sir, I'm sure,' said the landlord, ' but I'll soon put it right. Boy, bring another label!' An old story, I am afraid, but it seems to me to put Party goverment into a nutshell."

I rose, and began to replace the stoppers in the decanters. I was feeling rather cross. I hate having my settled convictions tampered with. They are not elastic, and this makes them brittle, and I always feel nervous about their stability when the intellectual pressure of an argument grows intense.

" When you two have abolished the British Constitution," I remarked tartly, " what do you propose to substitute for the present *regime?"*

" ' There,'" said Champion, " as the charwoman replied when asked for a character, ' you *'ave* me.' Let us join the ladies."

But I was still angry.

"It always seems best to me," I persisted doggedly, "to take up a good sound line of action and stick to it, and to choose a good sound party and stick to *that.* Half a glass of sherry before we go upstairs?"

"No, thanka That is why I envy you, Adrian," said Champion. " It's a wearingbusiness for us, being so – so – what shall we call it, Mr Fordyce ?"

" Detached ?" suggested Robin.

"That's it."

"Two-faced would be a better word," I growled.

Champion clapped me on the shoulder.

" Adrian," said he, " in time of peace there is always a large, critical, neutral, and infernally irritating party, for ever philandering betwixt and between two extremes of opinion. But when war is declared and it comes to a fight, the ranks close up. There is no room for detachment, and there are no neutrals. When occasion calls, you'll find all your friends – your half-hearted, carping, Erastian friends – ranged up tight beside you. Shall we be trapesing about in Tom Tiddler's ground when the pinch comes, Mr Fordyce – eh ? "

" Never fear !" said Robin.

And I am bound to say that we all of us lived to see John Champion's assertion made good.

3

SECTION 3

76

CHAPTER SIX.

ROBIN OFF DUTY.

I HAVE yet to introduce to the indulgent reader two more members of the family into which I have married.

The first of these is my daughter Phillis, of whom I have already made passing mention. She is six years old, and appears to be compounded of about equal parts of angelic innocence and original sin. In her dealings with her fellow-creatures she exhibits all the *sangfroid* and self-possession that mark the modern child. She will be a " handful" some day, the Twins tell me, and they ought to know. However, pending the arrival of the time when she will begin to rend the hearts of young men, she contents herself for the present with practising that accomplishment with complete and lamentable success upon her own garments.

She is the possessor of a vivid imagination, which she certainly does not inherit from me, and is fond of impersonating other people, either characters of her own creation or interesting figures from story-books. Consequently it is never safe to address her too suddenly. She may be a fairy, or a bear, or a locomotive at the moment, and will resent having to return to her proper self, even for a brief space, merely to listen to some stupid and irrelevant remark – usually something about bedtime or an open door – from an unintelligent adult.

Kitty says that I spoil her, but that is only because Kitty is quicker at saying a thing than I am. She is our only child; and I sometimes wonder, at moments of acute mental introspection (say, in the night watches after an indigestible supper), what we should do without her.

The other character waiting for introduction is my brother-in-law, Master Gerald Rubislaw. He is the solitary male member of the family of which my wife and the Twins form the female side. He is, I think, fourteen years of age, and he is at present a member of what he considers – very rightly, I think; and 1 should know, for I was there myself – the finest public school in the world. Having no parents, he resides at myhouse during his holidays, and refreshes me exceedingly.

He is a sturdy but rather diminutive youth, with a loud voice. (He always addresses me as if I were standing on a distant hill-top.) He bears a resemblance to his sisters of which he is heartily and frankly ashamed, and which he endeavours at times to nullify as far as possible by a degree of personal uncleanliness which would be alarming to me, were it not that the traditions of my own extreme youth have not yet been entirely obliterated from my memory.

His health is excellent, and his intellect is in that condition euphemistically described in house - master's reports as " unformed." He is always noisy, constitutionally lazy, and hopelessly casual. But he possesses the supreme merit of being absolutely and transparently honest. I have never known him tell a lie or do a mean thing. To such much is forgiven.

At present he appears to possess only two ambitions in life; one, to gain a place in his Junior House Fifteen, and the other, to score some signal and lasting victory over his form- master, a Mr Sydney Mellar, with whom he appears to wage a sort of perpetual guerillawarfare. Every vacation brings him home with a fresh tale of base subterfuges, petty tyrannies, and childish exhibitions of spite on the part of the infamous Mellar, all duly frustrated, crushed, and made ridiculous by the ingenuity, resource, and audacity of the intrepid Rubislaw. I have never met Mr Mellar in the flesh, but I am conscious, as time goes on and my young relative's reminiscences on the subject accumulate, of an increasing feeling of admiration and respect for him.

" He's a rotten brute," observed Gerald one day. "Do you know what he had the cheek to do last term?"

"What?"

"Well, there was a clinking new desk put into our form-room, at the back. I sit there," he added rather *naively.* "As soon as I saw it, of course I got out my knife and started to carve my name. I made good big letters, as I wanted to do the thing properly on a fine new desk like that."

" Was this during school hours ?" I ventured to inquire.

" Of course it was. Do you think a chap would be such a silly ass as to want to come in specially to carve his name during play-hours, when he's got the whole of his school-time to do it in?"

" I had not thought of that," I said apologetically.

"And don't go putting on side of that sort, Adrian, old man," roared Gerald, in what a stranger would have regarded as a most threatening voice, though I knew it was merely the one he keeps for moments of playful badinage. "I saw *your* name carved in letters about four inches high in the Fifth Form room only the other day. I don't see how you can jaw a man for doing a thing you used to do yourself thirty or forty years ago."

I allowed this reflection on my appearance to pass without protest, and Gerald resumed his story.

" Well, I did a first-class G to begin with, and was well on with the Bubislaw – all in capitals: I thought it would look best that way – when suddenly a great hand reached over my shoulder and grabbed my knife. It was Stinker, of course."

"St "

" Oh, I forgot to tell you that. We call him 'Stinker' now. You see, bis name is S. Mellar, and if you say it quickly it sounds like ' Smeller.'So we call him 'Stinker.' It was a kid called Lane thought of it. Pretty smart – eh ? Oh, he's a clever chap, I can tell you," yelled Gerald, with sincere enthusiasm.

" He must be a youth of gigantic intellect," I said.

"Oh, come off the roof! Well, Stinker grabbed my knife, and said, ' Hallo, young man, what's all this ? Handing down your name to posterity – eh ?' with a silly grin on his face.

" I said I was just carving my name.

" ' I see you have just finished it,' he said.

" I didn't quite tumble to his meaning at first, because I had only got as far as G. RUB, – and then I saw that the whole thing as it stood spelled ' GRUB.' Lord, how the swine laughed ! He told the form all about it, and of course they all laughed too, the sniggering, grovelling sweeps !

" Then Stinker said: ' A happy thought has just occurred to me. I shall not have your name obliterated in the usual manner' – they cut it out and put in a fresh bit of wood, and charge you a bob – ' this time. I have thought of a more excellent way.' (He always talks like that, in a sort of slow drawl.) ' We will leave your name exactly as you have carved it. But remember, young man, not another letter do you add to that name so long as you are a member of this school. A Grub you are, – a nasty little destructive Grub, – and a Grub you shall remain, so far as that desk is concerned, for all time. And if ever in future years you come down here as a distinguished Old Boy – say a K. C. B. or an Alderman, – remember to bring your numerous progeny' – oh, he's a sarcastic devil! – 'to this room, and show them what their papa once was !'

" Of course all the chaps roared again, at the idea of me with a lot of kids. But that wasn't all. He switched off *that* tap quite suddenly, and said –

"' Seriously, though, I am not pleased about this. Carving your name on a desk is not one of the seven deadly sins, but doing so when I have told you not to *is*. This silly street-boy business has been getting too prevalent lately: we shall have you chalking things up on the walls next. I particularly gave out last week, when this new desk was put in, that no one was to touch it. Come to me at twelve, and I will cane you.' And he *did*," concluded Gerald, with feeling.

" What a shame !" said Dilly, who was sitting by. " All for carving a silly old desk."

"He was perfectly right," said Gerald, his innate sense of justice rising to the surface at once. " I wasn't lammed for cutting the desk at all: it was for doing it after I had been told not to."

"It's the same thing," said Dilly, with feminine disregard for legal niceties.

" Same thing ? Rot! Fat lot you know about it, Dilly. It's a rum thing," he added to me in a reflective bawl, "but women never can understand the rules of any game. Stinker is a bargee, but he was quite right to lam me. It was for disobedience; and disobedience -is cheek; and no master worth his salt will stand cheek. So Stinker says, and he is right for

once."

Gerald is the possessor of a bosom friend, an excessively silent and rather saturnine youth of about his own age. His name is Donkin, and he regards Gerald, so far as I can see, with a grim mixture of amusement and compassion. He pays frequent visits to my house, as his father is a soldier in India; and he is much employed by the Twins for corroborating or refuting the more improbable of their brother's reminiscences.

Robin soon made friends with the boys. Like most of their kind, their tests of human probity were few and simple: and having discovered that Robin not only played Rugby football, but had on several occasions represented Edinburgh University thereat, they straightway wrote him down a " decent chap " and took the rest of his virtues for granted.

It came upon them – and me too, as a matter of fact – as rather a shock one evening, when Robin, during the course of a desultory conversation on education in general, suddenly launched forth *more suo* into a diatribe against the English Public School system.

English boys, he pointed out, were passed through a great machine, which ground up the individual at one end and disgorged a mere type at the other – ("Pretty good type too, Robin," from me), – they were taught to worship bodily strength – (" Quite right too!" said my herculean brother-in-law), – they were herded together under a monastic system; they were removed from the refining influence of female society – (even the imperturable Donkin snorted at this), – and worst of all, little or nothing was done to eradicate from their minds the youthful idea that it is unmanly to read seriously or think deeply.

I might have said a good deal in reply. I might have dwelt upon the fact that the English Public School system is not so hard upon the stupid boy – which means the average boy – as that of more strenuous forcing-houses of intellect abroad. I might have spoken of one or two moral agents which prevent our schools from being altogether despicable : unquestioning obedience to authority, for instance, or loyalty to tradition. I might have told of characters moulded and fibres stiffened by responsibility – our race bears more responsibility on its shoulders than all the rest of the world put together – or of minds trained to interpret laws and balance justice in the small but exacting world of the prefects' meeting and the games' committee. But it was Gerald, who is no moralist, but a youth of sound common-sense, who closed the argument.

"Mr Fordyce," he said, "it's no use *my* jawing to you, because you can knock me flat at that game; and of course old Moke there " – this was Master Donkin's unhappy but inevitable designation among his friends – "is too thick to argue with a stuffed rabbit; but you had better come down some time and *see* the place – that's all."

Robin promised to suspend judgment pending a personal investigation, and the incident closed.

Gerald's verdict on Robin's views, communicated to me privately afterwards, was characteristic but not unfavourable.

" He seems to have perfectly putrid notions about some things, but he's a pretty sound chap on the whole – the best secretary you have had, anyhow, old man. Have you seen him do a straight-arm balance on the billiard-table ?"

But I did not fully realise how completely Robin had settled down as an accepted member of my household until one afternoon towards the end of the Christmas holidays.

There is a small but snug apartment opening out of my library, through an arched and curtained doorway. The library is regarded as my workroom – impregnable, inviolable; not to be rudely attempted by devastating housemaids. There is a sort of tacit agreement between Kitty and myself as regards this apartment. Fatima-like, she may do what she pleases with the rest of the house. She may indulge her passion for drawing-room meetings to its fullest extent. She may entertain missionaries in the attics and hold meetings of the Dorcas Society in the basement. She maygive reformed burglars the run of the silver- closet, and allow curates and chorus-girls to mingle in sweet companionship on the staircase. But she must leave the library alone, and neither she nor her following must overflow through its double doors during what I call business hours.

On this particular afternoon I had been engaged upon the draft of a small bill with which I had been entrusted – we will call it the "Importation of Mad Dogs Bill," – and about four o'clock I handed it to Robin with instructions to write out a fair copy. Robin retired into his inner chamber, and I sat down in an arm-chair with *Punch.* (It was a Wednesday, the Parliamentary half-holiday of those days, and still, happily, the *Punch-d&y* of these.)

Kitty was holding a Drawing-room Meeting upstairs. I forget what description of body she was entertaining: it was either a Society for the Propagation of something which could never, in the nature of things, come to birth; or. else an Association for the Prevention of something that was bound to go on so long as the world endured. I had been mercifully absolved from attending, and my tea had been sent in to me. I was enjoying an excellent caricature of myChief in the minor cartoon of *Punch,* when I heard the door of the inner room open and the voice of my daughter inquire –

" Are you *drefful* busy, Uncle Robin ? " (My secretary had been elevated to avuncular rank after a probation of just three hours.)

There was a sound as of a chair being pushed back, and a rustle which suggested the hasty laying aside of a manuscript, and Robin's voice said –

" Come away, Philly 1" (This is a favourite Scoticism of Robin's, and appears to be a term denoting hearty welcome.)

There was a delighted squeal and the sound of pattering feet. Next ensued a period of rather audible osculation, and then there was silence. Presently Phillis said –

"What shall we do? Shall I sing you a hymn ? "

Evidently the revels were about to commence.

"I have just learned a new one," she continued. "I heared it in Church yesterday afternoon, so I brought it home and changed it a bit. It's called ' Onward, Chwistian Sailors !'"

"'*Soldiers*,' isn't it?"

"No – '*Sailors.*' It *was* 'Soldiers/ but I like sailors much better than soldiers, so I changed it. I'll sing it now."

"Wait till Sunday," said Robin, with much presence of mind. " Will you not tell me a story ?"

This idea appeared so good that Phillis began forthwith.

" Once there were three horses what lived in a stable. Two was wise and one was just a foolish young horse. There was some wolves what lived quite near the stable "

"Wolves?" said my secretary, in tones of mild surprise.

" The stable," explained Phillis, " stood in the midst of the snowy plains of Muscovy. I should have telled you that before."

" Just so," said Robin gravely. " Go on."

" Well, one day," continued the narratress's voice through the curtains – I knew the story by heart, so I was able to fill up the gaps for myself when she dropped to a confidential whisper – "one cold, windy, berleak day, the old wolves said to the young ones, 'How about a meal of meat ?' and all the young one's said, 'Oh, *let's!*'

" That very morning," continued Phillis in the impressive bass which she reserves for the most exciting parts of her narrative, "that *very* morning the foolish young horse said to theold horses, 'Who is for a scamper to-day?' Then he began to wiggle and wiggle at his halter. The old horses said, ' There is wolves outside, and our master says that they eat all sheep an' cattle an' horses.' But the young horse just wiggled and wiggled," – I could hear my daughter suiting the action to the word upon her audience's knee, – " and pwesently his halter was off! Then out he rushed, kicking up the nimble snow with his feathery heels, and – what ? "

Robin, who was automatically murmuring something about transferred epithets, apologised for this pedantic lapse, and the tale proceeded.

" Well, just as he was goin' to have one more scamper, he felt a growl – a awful, fearful, deep *growl*" – Phillis's voice sank to a bloodcurdling and continuous gurgle – " and he terrembled, like this! I'll show you "

She slipped off Eobin's knee, and I knew that she was now on the hearth-rug, simulating acute palsy for his benefit.

"Then he felt somefing on his back, then somefing further up his back, then a bite at his neck; and then he felt his head bitten off, and he died. Now you tell me one."

" Which ?"

Phillis considered.

"The one about the Kelpie and the Wee Bit Lassie."

Robin obliged. At first he stumbled a little, and had to be prompted in hoarse whispers by Phillis (who apparently had heard the story several times before); but as the narrative progressed and the adventures of the wee bit lassie grew more enthralling and the Kelpie more terrifying, he became almost as immersed as his audience. When I peeped through the curtain they were both sitting on the hearthrug pressed close together, Phillis gripping one of Robin's enormous hands in a pleasurable condition of terrified interest. The fair copy of the "Importation of Mad Dogs Bill," I regret to say, lay on the floor under the table. I retired to my arm-chair.

" The Kelpie," Robin continued, " came closer and closer behind her. Already she could feel a hot breath on her neck." (So could Robin on his, for that matter.) "But she did not give in. She ran faster and faster until "

" You've forgotten to say she could hear its webbed feet going *pad pad* over the slippery stanes," interpolated Phillis anxiously.

"So I did. I'm sorry. She could hear its webbed feet going *pad pad* over the slipperystanes. Presently though, she came to a wee bit housie on the moor. It was empty, but she slippit through the yard-gate and flew along the path and in at the door. The Kelpie came flying through the gate "

" No, no – it loupit ower the dyke!" screamed Phillis, who would countenance no tamperings with the original text.

"Oh, yes. It loupit ower the dyke, but the wee lassie just slammed the door in its face, and turned the key. Then she felt round in the dark and keeked about, wondering what kind of place she was in. And at that very moments through a bit window in the wall "

"She went ben first."

" Oh, yes. She went ben; and at that very moment, through the bit window in the back- end of the house, there came a ray of light. The sun "

" The sun had risen," declaimed Phillis, triumphantly taking up the tale; " and with one wild sheriek of disappointed rage the Kelpie vanished away, and the wee lassie was *saved.'"*

There was a rapt pause after this exciting anecdote. Then Phillis remarked –

"Uncle Bobin, let's write that story down, and then I can get people to read it to me."

"Why not write it down for yourself?"

"I can't write – much; and it ought to be writed in ink, and I – I am only allowed to use pencil," explained my daughter, not without a certain bitterness. " But I put the lead in my mouf," she added defiantly.

At this moment the door of my apartment was hurled open, and Gerald projected himself into the room. It was the evening before his return to school, and there was a predatory look in his eye. He was accompanied by his speechless friend.

"Adrian, old son," he began, in such tones as an orator might address to a refractory mob, "Moke and I are going to have a study next term, and we want some furniture."

I mildly remarked that in my day furniture was supplied by the school authorities.

"Yes, but I mean pictures and things. Can you give us one ? We shall want something to go on that wall opposite the window, shan't we, Moke ? The place where young Lee missed your head with the red-ink bottle. *Have* you got a picture handy, Adrian?"

I replied in the negative.

Gerald took not the slightest notice.

" It will have to be a pretty big one," hecontinued. "There is a good lot of red ink to cover. I have been taking a look round the house, and I must say the pictures you've got are a fairly mangy lot – aren't they, Moke ?"

The gentleman addressed coughed depre- catingly, and looked at me as much as to say that, whatever he thought of my taste in art, he had eaten my salt and would refrain from criticism.

"There's one that might do, though," continued Gerald. "It's hanging in the billiard-room – a big steamer in a storm."

By this time Phillis and Robin had joined the conclave.

" I know," said Phillis, nodding her head; "a great beautiful boat in some waves. I should fink it was a friend of the *Great Eastern's,* " she added, referring to an antiquated print of the early Victorian leviathan which hung in the nursery.

" We could take it for a term or two, anyhow," continued Gerald, "until we get something better. I'm expecting some really decent ones after summer. Ainslie *major* is leaving then, and he has promised to let me have some of his cheap. Then you can have yours back, Adrian. That's the scheme 1 Come on. Moke, we'll go and take it down now. Thanks very much, old chap " (to me). " I'll tell Kitty that you've let us. We can jab it off its hook with a billiard - cue, I should think, Moke. Come too, will you, Mr Fordyce? You can stand underneath and catch it, in case it comes down with a run. So long, Adrian!"

The whole pack of them swept from the room, leaving the door open.

When I looked in at the billiard - room on my way up to dress for dinner an hour later, nothing remained to mark the spot hitherto occupied by a signed and numbered proof of *An Ocean Greyhound,* by Michael Angelo Mahlstaff, A. E.. A. (a wedding gift to my wife and myself from the artist), but the imprints of several hot hands on the wall, together with a series of parallel perpendicular scars, apparently inflicted by a full-sized harrow.

From which two chapters it will be gathered that Robert Chalmers Fordyce was a man capable, in his ordinary working-day, of playing many parts.

CHAPTER SEVEN.

A DISSOLUTION OP PARTNERSHIP.

My wife and I would have been more than human if we had not occasionally cast a curious eye upon the relations of Robin and the Twins.

Of Robin's attitude towards that pair of charmers Kitty could make little and I nothing. He kept his place and went his own way – rather ostentatiously, I thought – and appeared if anything to avoid them. If he found himself in their company he treated them with a certain grave reticence – he soon grew out of his fondness for addressing us like a public meeting – and made little attempt to bestow upon them the attentions which young maidens are accustomed to receive from young men.

There was no mystery about the Twins' attitude towards Robin. "Here," said they ineffect, "is *a,* fine upstanding young man, full of promise, but hampered in every direction by abysmal ignorance on matters of vital importance. His instincts are sound, but at present he is quite impossible. What he wants is mothering."

And so they mothered him, most maternally. They exerted themselves quite stren-uously to instil into him the fundamental principles of life – the correct method of tying a dress tie; the intricate ritual which governs such things as visiting-cards and asparagus; the exact limit of the domains of brown boots and dinner-jackets; the utter criminality of dickeys, turn-down collars, and side-whiskers; and the superiority of dialogue to monologue as a concomitant to afternoon tea.

In many respects, they discovered with pleased surprise, their pupil required no instruction or surveillance. For instance, he could always be trusted to enter or leave a room without awkwardness, and his manner of address was perfect. He was neither servile nor familiar, and the only people to whom I ever saw him pay marked deference were the members of what is after all the only real and natural aristocracy in the world – that of old age.

All their ministrations Robin received with grave wonder – he was not of the sort that can easily magnify a fetish into a deity – but, evidently struck by the intense importance attached by the Twins to their own doctrines, he showed himself a most amenable pupil. Probably he realised, in spite of hereditary preference for inward worth as opposed to outward show,, that though a coat cannot make a man, a good man in a good coat often has the advantage of a good man in a bad coat. So he allowed the Twins to round off his corners; and, without losing any of his original ruggedness of character or toughness of fibre, he soon developed into a well-groomed and sufficiently presentable adjunct – quite distinguished-looking, Dilly said, when she met us one day on our way down to the House – to a lady's morning walk.

What he really thought of it all I do not know. I have a kind of suspicion that deep down in his heart every Scot entertains a contempt for the volatile and frivolous English which is only equalled by that of the English for the nation to whom I once heard a Highland minister refer as "the giddy and godless French"; but Robin was not given to the revelation of his privatethoughts. He seldom spoke of the Twins to me – he was a discusser of manners rather than men – but he once remarked that they were girls of widely different character. He entered into no further details, but I remember being struck by the observation at the tune; for I had always regarded my sisters-in-law as being as identical in disposition as they were in appearance.

Still it was pretty to see Eobin unbending to please the two girls, and to hear him say " No, really ? " or " My word, what rot!" when you knew that his tongue was itching to cry, " Is that a fact ?" or " Hoots !" or " Havers !" as the occasion demanded.

He also possessed the great and unique merit of not being ashamed to ask for guidance in a difficulty. I have known him pause before an unfamiliar dish at table and ask one of his preceptresses, in the frankest manner possible, whether the exigencies of the situation called for a spoon or a fork: and out of doors it was a perpetual joy to hear him whisper, on the approach of some one whoni he thought might be a friend of ours, "Will I lift my hat?"

All that year Eobin was my right hand. Itwas a long session; and as my Chief sat in the Upper House, much work in the way of answering questions and making statements fell upon me. We had a good working majority, but the Opposition were a united and well-organised body that year, and we had to rise early and go to bed late to keep their assaults at bay while proceeding with the programme of the session. Every afternoon, before I entered the House to take my place at question-time, my secretary insisted on taking me through the answers which he had prepared for my recitation ;

and we also discussed the line of action to be pursued if I were cornered by questions of the " arising-out-of-that-answer " order.

Personally, I loathed this part of the work – I am a departmentalist pure and simple – but Robin's eye used to glow with the light of battle as he rehearsed me in the undoubtedly telling counters with which I was to pulverise the foe.

" I would like fine," he once said to me, " to stand up in your place and answer these questions for you."

" I wish you could, Robin," I sighed. " And," I added, "I believe you will some day." Robin turned pink'for the first time in our acquaintance, and I heard his teeth click suddenly together.

So the wind lay that way 1

During the next year my household was furnished with three surprises, Dilly contributing one and Robin two.

Robin's came first. One was his uncle, the other his book.

One night it fell to my lot to dine in the City, as the guest of the Honourable Company of Tile- Glazers and Mortar-Mixers. As I swam forlornly through a turgid ocean of turtle-soup and clarified punch towards an unyielding continent of fish, irrigated by brown sherry, mechanically rehearsing to myself the series of sparkling yet statesmanlike epigrams with which I proposed to reply to the toast of his Majesty's Ministers, I became aware that the gentleman on my left was addressing me in a voice that seemed vaguely familiar.

"And how is my brother's second boy doing with you, Mr Inglethwaite ? "

I must have looked a trifle blank, for he added –

"My nephew, Robin."

I glanced obliquely at the card which marked his place at table, and read –

Sir James Fordyce.

Then I began to grasp the situation, and I realised that this great man, whose name was honourably known wherever the ills of childhood are combated, was Robin's uncle, the "doctor" to whom my secretary had casually referred, and whom he occasionally went to visit on Sunday afternoons. I had pictured an overdriven G. P., living in Bloomsbury or Bal– ham, with a black bag, and a bulge in his hat where he kept his stethoscope. A man sufficiently distinguished to represent his profession at a public banquet was more than I had bargained for.

We became friends at once, and supported each other, so to speak, amid the multitude of dinners and dishes, our respective neighbours proving but broken reeds so far as social intercourse was concerned. On Sir James's left, I remember, sat a plethoric gentleman whose burnished countenance gave him the appearance of a sort of incarnate Glazed Tile; while my right-hand neighbour, from the manner in which he manipulated the food upon his plate, I put down without hesitation as a Mortar Mixer of high standing.

The old gentleman gave me a good deal of information about Robin.

" He had a hard fight his first year or two in London," he said. " I could see by the way he fell upon his dinner when he came to my house that his meat and drink were not easily come by. Still, now that he has won through, he will not regret the experience. I had it myself. It is the finest training that a young man can receive.

Hard, terribly hard, but invaluable ! You will not have seen his father yet – my brother John?"

I told him no.

"Well, try and meet him. You, as an Englishman, would perhaps call him hard and narrow, – after forty years of London I sometimes find him so myself, – but he is a fine man, and he has a good wife. So have you,"he added unexpectedly – "Robin *has* told me that."

I laughed, in what the Twins call the "silly little gratified way" which obtrudes itself into my demeanour when any one praises Kitty.

"I hope you are in the same happy situation," I said.

"No, I am a bachelor. My brother John has not achieved a K. C. B., but he is a more fortunate man than I."

The conversation dropped here, but I repeated it to my wife afterwards.

"Of course, the whole thing is as clear as daylight," she said. " These two brothers both wanted to marry the same girl She took the farmer one, so the other, poor thing, went off to London and became a famous doctor instead. That's all. He might have been Robin's father, but he's only his uncle."

Happy the mind which can reconstruct a romance out of such scanty material.

Sir James ultimately dined at my house, and became a firm friend of all that dwelt therein, especially Fhillis.

Then came Robin's second surprise – his book. It was a novel, and a very good novel too. Hehad been at it for some time, he told me, but it was only recently that he had contrived to finish it off. Being distrustful of its merits, he had decided to offer it to just one good publisher, who could take it or leave it. If he took it, well and good. But if the publisher (and possibly just one other) exhibited an attitude of aloofness, Robin had fully decided not to hawk his bantling about among other less reputable and more amenable firms, but to consign it to his bedroom fire.

However, this inhuman but only-too-unusual sacrifice of the parental instinct was averted by the one good publisher, who accepted the book, and introduced Robin to the public.

Either through shyness or indifference Robin had told us nothing of the approaching interesting event, and it was not until one morning in October, when a parcel of complimentary copies arrived from the publisher's, that we were apprised of the fact that we had been cherishing an author in our midst. Robin solemnly presented us with a copy apiece (which I thought handsome but extravagant), and also sent one to his parents, who, though I think they rather doubted the propriety of possessinga son who wrote novels at all, wrote back comparing it very favourably with *The Pilgrim's Progress,* the only other work of fiction with which they were acquainted.

The book itself dealt with matters rather than men, and with men rather than women; which was characteristic of its author, but rather irritating for the Twins. It had a good deal to say about the under-side of journalism, – graphic and convincing, all this, – and contained a rather technical but absorbingly interesting account of some most exciting financial operations, winding up with a great description of a panic on the Stock Exchange. But there were few light and no tender passages, from which it will be seen that Robin as an author appealed to the male rather than the female intellect.

The Twins, I think, were secretly rather disappointed with the book, less from any particular fondness for the perusal of love-passages than from a truly human desire to note how Robin would have handled them; for it is always interesting to see to what extent our friends will give themselves away when they commit the indiscretion of a book. On this occasion Robin had been exasperatingly self-contained.

But life is full of compensations. There was a dedication. It read : –

THIS BOOK
OWES ITS INCEPTION,
AND IS THEREFORE
DEDICATED,
TO
A CIRCUMSTANCE
OVER
WHOM
I HAVE NO CONTROL.
R C. V.

Now it is obvious that in nine cases out of ten there is only one circumstance over whom a vigorous young man has no control, and this circumstance wears petticoats. Hitherto I had not seriously connected Robin with the tender passion, and this sudden intimation that the most serious - minded and ambitious of young men is not immune from the same rather startled me.

The female members of my establishment were pleasantly fluttered, though they were concerned less with the lady's existence than with her identity.

"Who do you think she is?" inquired Kitty of me, the first time the subject cropped up between us.

"Don't know, I'm sure," I murmured. I was smoking my post - prandial cigar at the time, at peace with all the world. "Never had the privilege of seeing his visiting-list."

"I wonder who she *can* be," continued my wife. " He – he hasn't said anything to you, has he, dear?" she inquired, in a tentative voice.

I slowly opened one of my hitherto closed eyes, and cocked it suspiciously at the diplomatist sitting opposite to me. (The Twins and Robin were out at the theatre.) Then, observing that she was stealthily regarding me through her eyelashes – a detestable trick which some women have – I solemnly agitated my eyelid some three or four times and gently closed it again.

"Has he confided any of his love affairs to you, I mean ?" continued Kitty, quite unabashed.

" If you eat any more chocolates you will make yourself sick," I observed.

" Yes, dear," said my wife submissively, pushing away the bon-bon dish. " But has he ?"

" Are you trying to pump me ?"

" Oh, gracious, no! What would be the good ? I only asked a plain question. You men are such creatures for screening each other, though, that it's never any use asking a man anything about another man."

"True for you. As a matter of fact, Robin has hardly said a word to me on the subject of women since first I met him."

Kitty thoughtfully cracked a filbert with her teeth – an unladylike habit about which I have often spoken to her – and said –

" What exciting chats you must have t Then she added reflectively –

" I expect it's a girl in Scotland. A sort of Highland lassie, in a kilt, or whatever female Highlanders wear."

"Why should a novel about the Stock Exchange ' owe its inception' to a Highland lassie ? "

Kitty took another filbert.

"That's 'vurry bright' of you, Adrian, as that American girl used to say. There's something in that. (Yes, I know you don't like it, dear, but I love doing it. I'll pour you out another glass of port. There!) But any idiotic excuse is good enough for a man in love. Has he ever been sentimental with you – quoted poetry, or anything?"

"N-no. Stop, though! He did once quote Burns to me, but that was & *propos* of poetry in general, not of love-making."

I remembered the incident well. Robin had picked up at a bookstall a copy of an early and quite valuable edition of Burns' poems. He had sat smoking with me in the library late the same night, turning over the pages of the tattered volume, and quoting bits, in broad vernacular, from "Tarn o' Shanter" and "The Cotter's Saturday Night." Suddenly he began, almost to himself" –

" O, my love is like a red, red rose,
That's newly sprung in June;
My love is like a melody
That's sweetly played in tune.
As fair art thou, my bonnie lass,
So deep in love am I "

He broke off for a moment, and I remembered how he glowered ecstatically into the fire. Then he concluded –

"And I will love thee still, my dear,
Till a' the seas gang dry."

" Man," he said, " that's fine ! That's poetry. That's the real thing!"

I had agreed. It is no use arguing with a Scot about Burns. (I remember once beingnearly dirked at a Caledonian Dinner because I ventured to remark that "before ye" was not in my opinion a good rhyme to "Loch Lomond.")

However, Kitty and I were unable to decide whether Robin's " bonnie lass" on that occasion had been a personality or an abstraction.

"Mightn't it be one of the Twins?" I remarked.

" Well, it *might* be," admitted Kitty judicially, "but he has kept it very close if it is. No," she continued more decidedly, " I don't think it *can* be. They are quite out of his line. Besides – it would be too absurd !"

It was not one Twin at any rate, for a fortnight later Dilly sprung upon us the third surprise of the series I have mentioned. She announced that she had decided to marry Dicky Lever.

There was, I suppose, nothing very surprising in that. Dicky had been in constant attendance upon the Twins for nearly two years, and had long since graduated into the ranks of the Good Sorts. The surprise to us – rather unreasonably, perhaps – lay in the fact of –

1. Dicky having definitely fixed upon a particular Twin to propose to;

2. That Twin having definitely selected Dicky out of the assortment at her command.

I was so accustomed to seeing my sisters- in-law compassed about by a cloud of young men who appeared to admire them both equally, and to whom they appeared to apportion their favours with indiscriminate *camaraderie,* that the idea of one admirer stealing a march on all the others seemed a little unfair, somehow.

As Dolly remarked, it would break up the firm horribly.

"You see," she confided to me rather plaintively, " Dilly will have no use for them now, and they'll have still less use for her – an engaged girl beside other girls is about as exciting as a tapioca - pudding at a Lord Mayor's Banquet – and they will only have me. That won't be half the fun."

"I should have thought that your fun would have been exactly doubled," I said.

" Not a bit. How like a man ! Don't you see, the fun used to be in playing them backwards and forwards between our two selves – like ping-pong, you know 1 It was clinking !"

She sighed regretfully.

"Now I shall either have to avoid men or marry them," she concluded, vaguely butregretfully. "Before, if they got in the way, I could always volley them back to Dilly. Now – one can't play ping-pong all by oneself 1"

IIL

Billy's engagement, as is usual under such circumstances, afforded my household many opportunities for airy badinage and innocent merriment.

Dolly always heralded her coming into the billiard - room, where the affianced pair had staked out a claim, by a cough of penetrating severity, and usually entered the room with her features obscured by an open umbrella. On several occasions, too, she impersonated her sister; and once, when Dicky was spending a week-end in the house, was only prevented by the fraction of a second from robbing that incensed damosel of her morning salute.

My share in the proceedings was limited to a single constrained interview with Dicky, at which, feeling extremely rude and inquisitive, I asked him the usual stereo-typed questions about his income, prospects, and habits (most

of which I knew only too well already), which, being satisfactorily answered, I rang the bell for the Tantalus, and thanked heaven that the Twins were not Triplets. I had indeed suggested that Dilly's nearest and most natural protector was her brother, Master Gerald, and that Dicky should apply not for my consent but his. This motion, however, was negatived without a division. I was sorry, for I think my brother-in-law would have shown himself worthy of the occasion.

My wife received the news of the engagement with all the enthusiasm usually exhibited by a Salvation lassie when a fresh convert is hustled forward to the " saved" bench, and henceforth divided her time between ordering Dilly's trousseau and giving tea-parties, at which the prospective bridegroom was produced and passed round, "as if," to use his own expression, "he were the newest thing in accordion-pleating."

As regards Robin's share in the event, I can only recall one incident. He had been away at Stoneleigh, the largest town in my constituency, on some party business, and when he returned home the engagement had been announced for nearly a week.

" I must go and offer my good wishes to MissDilly," he said, after hearing the news. "Do you know where she is, Mrs Inglethwaite ?"

"I saw her upstairs a few minutes ago," said Kitty. "Come up, and we'll find her."

We were in the library at the time, and Kitty and Robin left the room together. The rest of the story my wife told me later.

" We went up," she said, " and looked into the drawing-room, where I had last seen Dilly. The room was nearly dark, but she was there, sitting curled up in front of the fire.

" ' There she is,' I said. ' Go and say something nice.'

" Well, dear," – Kitty's face assumed an air of impressive solemnity which makes her absurdly like her daughter – "he stood hesitating a moment, and then walked straight up to her and said –

" ' Good afternoon ! Can you tell me where your sister is ? I want to offer her my good wishes on the great event.'

" It wasn't Dilly at all. It was Dolly! And he was able to distinguish between the two in that dim room. And / couldn't!"

" Oh," said I carelessly, " I expect he noticed she wasn't wearing an engagement-ring."

My wife looked at me and sighed, as over

one who would spoil & romance for want of a ha'porth of sentiment. And yet I know she would have been quite scandalised if any one had hinted at tender passages between her sister and my secretary. Women are curious creatures.

4

SECTION 4

CHAPTER EIGHT.
  OF A PIT THAT WAS DIGGED, AND WHO
  FELL INTO IT.

Dicky Lever was a hearty and not particularly intellectual youth of the What ho! type (if you know what I mean). He was employed in some capacity in a Government office, but his livelihood was not entirely dependent on his exertions therein – which was, perhaps, fortunate, as his sole claim to distinction in his Department lay in the fact of his holding the record for the highest score at small cricket in the Junior Secretaries' room. He was a member of the Leander Club, a more than usually capable amateur actor, and a very good fellow all round. The engagement was announced at the end of July, which is a busy time for this country's legislators. The session was drawing to a close, and we were passing Bills with a prodigality and despatch which provoked many not altogether undeserved gibes from a reptile Opposition Press concerning the devotion of his Majesty's Government to the worship of Saint Grouse.

One night I brought Champion home to dinner between the afternoon and evening sittings. At the latter he was to move the second reading of his " Municipal Co-ordination Bill," a measure which was intended to grapple with the chaos arising from the multitude of opposing or overlapping interests that controlled the domestic arrangements of the Londoner. An effort was to be made to bring all the Gas, Electricity, Water, Paving, and other corporations into some sort of line, and prevent them from getting into each other's way and adding to the expenses and inconvenience of the much-enduring ratepayer. It was a useful little Bill; but though everybody approved of it on principle, various powerful interests were at work against it, and its prospects of getting through Committee hung in the balance.

"Now, Mr Champion," said Dilly, who knew that a man always likes to be questioned about his work, especially by a pretty girl, "what will your Bill do for *us? I* have asked this person here," – indicating her *Jiancó,* – " but hesays parish-pump politics aren't in his department. He licks stamps at the Foreign Office," she added in explanation.

"Tell her, Champion," said Dicky. "Out of my line altogether. Takes me all my time to keep an eye on those Johnnies in the Concert of Europe."

"I will tell you one thing the Bill will do, Miss Dilly," said Champion, a little heavily. (Dolly once said of him, " He's awfully clever and able and all that, but he hasn't got a light hand for conversational pastry.") " How many times have you noticed the streets up about here this year?"

"Heaps," said Dilly.

"They have hardly ever been down," corroborated Dolly.

" Let me see," continued Dilly. " Our side of the Square was repaved in January. Directly after that they took it up again and did something to the drains."

" In March they opened it again to lay down an electric light main," said I.

"In April something burst," said Dolly, "and that meant more men with wigwams and braziers."

"And last month," concluded Dilly, "theytook away the wood pavement and relaid the whole Square with some new patent asphalte, which smelt simply, oh "

" Rotten !" supplied Gerald. (Have I mentioned that he had just arrived home for his summer holiday ?)

"Well," said Champion, "the Bill would regulate that sort of thing. It would protect the streets from being torn up at will by any Company who happened to have business underneath them. As things are, practically any one may come along and hew holes anywhere he pleases."

"The police ought to stop it," said Kitty, who has a profound belief in the Force. (I am convinced that if Beelzebub himself were to enter the house at any time during my absence, Kitty would lure him into the dining- room with the sherry, and then telephone for a constable.)

"The police have no right," said Champion. " If a gas company choose to give notice that they intend on a certain day to come and burrow in a road, all the police can do is to divert the traffic, and make the gas company as comfortable as possible."

I was not following this conversation withany particular interest. Being expected to speak in favour of the Bill that night, I was undergoing the preliminary anguish which invariably attends my higher oratorical efforts. But I remember now that about this time Dilly suddenly turned to Dicky and whispered something in his ear. Then they both looked across the dinner-table at Robin, who nodded, as who should say,

"I know fine what you whispered then." After that they all three laughed and looked down the table at Champion, who was still expatiating on the merits of his Bill.

I suppose anybody else would have divined what was in the wind, but I did not.

A week later we were treated to an all-night sitting. The Irishmen had been quiescent of late, but on this occasion they made amends for their temporary relaxation of patriotism by resolutely obstructing an Appropriation Bill, which had to pass through Committee that night (if John Bull was to have any ready cash at all during the next few months), and kept us replying to amendments and trotting through division-lobbies until six o'clock next morning.

Robin stayed on in attendance at the House most of the night, but about three o'clock I sent him home, with instructions to stay in bed till tea-time if he pleased. He had had a hard time lately.

I was walking homeward in the early sunshine, marvelling, as people who accidentally find themselves up early pharisaically do, at the fatuity of those who waste the best hours of the whole day in bed, and revelling in the near prospect of a bath and my breakfast, when on turning a corner I walked into a hand-cart which was standing across the pavement. It contained workmen's tools – picks, shovels, and the like. On the near side of the roadway a man was erecting one of those curious wigwam arrangements which screen the operations of electricians and other subterranean burrowers from the public gaze. A dirty-faced small boy in corduroys was tending a brazier of live coals, upon which some breakfast cans were steaming. Between the wigwam and the pavement a gigantic navvy was hewing wooden paving- blocks out of the roadway.

The spectacle did not attract my interest specially, as this particular piece of street had been eviscerated so often that I had grown callous to its sufferings. But I paused for amoment to survey the big navvy's muscles, and to wonder how early in the morning it would be necessary to rise in order to catch a small boy with a clean face. The navvy was a fine specimen of humanity, with a complexion tanned a dusky coffee colour.

I was reflecting on the joys of the simple life and the futility of politics and other indoor pastimes in general, when the big man rose from his stooping posture and caught my eye. He appeared a little disconcerted by my scrutiny, and turned his back and renewed his exertions with increased vigour, favouring me hereafter with what architects call a "south elevation" of himself.

I went home to breakfast, wondering where I had seen the big navvy's back before. I mentioned casually to Kitty and the Twins that Goring Street was up again. They wondered how the management of the Goring Hotel liked it, with that mess under their very windows, and agreed with me that it was high time Champion's Bill, due for its Third Beading to-morrow, became law.

I stayed in bed till lunch - time, and then, rather late in the afternoon, set out for the House, which I knew I should find in anextremely limp condition after its previous night's dissipation. On the way I called in at the Goring Hotel in Goring Street, where Champion lived when in town. I found him in his room on the first floor, gazing out of the window into the street.

I looked out too, to see what was interesting him. Directly below us lay the encampment of the workmen whom I had seen in the morning. They had hewed up a few yards of the wood pavement, and the smaller of the two men was now immersed up to his waist in a hole, working rather laboriously in the restricted space at his command with a pick-axe. The boy was piling wooden blocks into a neat heap, and the big man, whose form was only partially visible, was doing something inside the wigwam.

The roadway was more than half blocked, and cabs and omnibuses, in charge of over-heated and eloquent drivers, were being filtered through the narrow space left at their disposal by a phlegmatic policeman.

"Look here," said Champion.

I looked.

" What on *earth* are those fellows doing ? " he continued.

" Re-laying the road, perhaps."

" One doesn't re-lay a road by making a deep hole in it."

"Well – gas !"

"Gas and electric light mains in this street are all led along a special conduit reached by manholes every eighty yards," said Champion. "There's no need to dig."

" Well – drains!" said I vaguely. But I was a mere child in the hands of this expert.

" The drains, as you call them," he said testily, "consist of a great sewer away in the depths, accessible from various appointed places. Besides, nobody in his senses tries to lift earth out of a hole with a pick-axe."

" Perhaps the solution of the mystery lies inside the wigwam," I said.

" No. That is just what complicates matters. When a shaft leading down to the electric light mains is opened, one of those canvas shelters is put over the top. Now there is *nothing* under that shelter – nothing but the bit of road it covers. The thing seems to be simply a stage accessory, planted there to give the encampment an aspect of reality. Ah, look at that!"

" That" was a small piece of paving-wood, dexterously hurled by the dirty-faced boy, who seemed to be finding time hang rather heavily on his hands. It took a passing citizen in the small of the back, but when he swung round to detect the source of the missile the boy was on his knees again industriously blowing up the brazier.

With an indignant snort the citizen passed on his way, doubtless adding the outrage, in his mind, to the long list of unsolved London crimes. But retribution awaited the youthful miscreant. The phlegmatic policeman who was regulating the traffic on the single-line system happened to notice the deed. He walked majestically across from the far side of the street towards our excavating friends.

" Come on !" said Champion to me. " There's going to be some fun."

We stepped out through one of the windows, which possessed a broad balcony, and took our stand behind some laurels in tubs which lined the balustrade. The street was comparatively quiet at the time, and we were able to hear most of the dialogue that ensued.

" 'Ere, mate," began the traffic-expert to the smaller of the two navvies, "just ketch that boy of yours a clip on the side of the 'ead, will you ? "

The smaller man desisted from his labours in the hole.

" Wotsye, ole sport ? " he inquired cheerily.

The policeman was a little ruffled by this familiarity.

" I'll trouble *you*," he repeated with some hauteur, " to ketch that boy of yours a clip on the side of the 'ead. If not, *I* shall 'ave to do my duty, according "

Here the roar of a passing dray drowned his utterance.

The smaller man clambered nimbly out of the hole and proceeded to grab his young friend by the scruff of the neck.

"Billy," he remarked dispassionately, "this gentleman says as 'ow I'm to give you a clip on the side of the 'ead."

" Woffor," inquired Billy, simulating extreme terror.

The man passed the question on to the policeman, who explained the nature of the offence. His statement was voluntarily corroborated by several members of an audience which seemed to have materialised from nowhere, and now formed a ring round the encampment.

" Righto!" said the man with cheery acquiescence. " Billy, my lad, you've got to 'ave it."

"Tha's right, ole son! You give 'im socks," remarked a hoarse and rather indistinct voiceof the gin-and-fog variety, from among the spectators.

Simultaneously its owner lurched his way to the front rank, the others making room for him with that respectful sympathy, not unmixed with envy, which is always accorded to a true-born Briton in his condition. He was obviously a member of some profession connected with coal- dust, and it was plain that he had been celebrating the conclusion of his day's labours.

The smaller navvy, thus exhorted, administered the desired clip. It was not a particularly severe one, but it drew from its recipient the somewhat unexpected expostulation –

"You silly ass! Not so hard!"

Where had I heard that stentorian but childish voice before? Who was this road-breaker's acolyte, with his brazier, his dirty face, and – a public-school accent?

I leaned over the balustrade and surveyed him and his two companions. Then I drew my breath sharply.

Merciful heavens 1

The dirty-faced boy was my brother-in-law, Master Gerald Eubislaw, the clip-administerer was Dicky Lever, and the gigantic and taciturn navvy was – my Secretary I

Having witnessed the carrying-out of the sentence, the policeman returned to his duties; none too soon; for a furniture van and a butcher's cart, locked in an inextricable embrace, the subject of a sulphurous duet between their respective proprietors, called loudly for his attention.

Meanwhile Coaldust, who had been inspecting the result of our friends' united labours with some interest, suddenly echoed the question which had first exercised Champion's logical mind by inquiring what the blank dash the two adjectival criminals and the qualified nipper thought they were doing to the asterisked road.

He received no encouragement. Robin was now engaged with a hammer and chisel in cutting a sort of touch-line all round the encampment, while Dicky did not cease manfully to delve with the pick-axe in the pit which he had digged for himself. For a long time they turned a deaf ear to the anxious inquiries of their interlocutor.

But there are limits to long-suffering. Coal- dust's witticisms increased with his audience, and at last Dicky turned to Robin and cried, with a really admirable maintenance of character and accent –

" 'Ere, Scotty, come and give this bloke one in the neck. 'E's askin' for it!"

Robin deliberately suspended operations, rose heavily to his feet, and cleared his throat. Then he turned upon the alcoholic Coaldust. I strained my ears. Surely *he* was not going to talk Cockney!

Far from it. He stuck to his last.

" See here, ma man," he roared, in a voice that made the crowd jump, "are ye for a ding on the side o' the heid?"

Coaldust capitulated with alacrity.

" No offence, 'Grace!" he remarked genially. "You an' me was always pals. Put it there!" He extended an ebony hand, which Robin solemnly shook and returned to his work.

Whatever my three friends were up to, it is possible that they might now have been left in peace for some time; for the crowd, seeing no chance of further sport from Coaldust, began to melt away. But a fresh character entered the scene to keep alive the flagging interest of the drama.

My first intimation that something new was afoot came from an errand - boy on the edge of the crowd, who, addressing a lady or ladies unseen, suddenly expressed a desire to be chased.

All heads were now turned down the street, and there, approaching with rather faltering steps, carrying a red cotton bundle and a tea- can, I beheld – one of my sisters-in-law!

Postulating Dicky, I presumed it was Dilly, and I began to piece together in my mind the plot of this elaborate comedy. Evidently Dicky, Robin, and Gerald had decided – for a bet, or because they were dared, or possibly with a view to giving Champion's Bill a leg-up by a practical demonstration of the crying need for it – to dress themselves up as workmen and come and "do a turn," as they say in the music halls, to the discomfort of his Majesty's lieges and the congestion of traffic, upon some sufficiently busy thoroughfare for a stated period of time.

Certainly they were doing it rather well. They were admirably made up, – Dicky was a past-master at that sort of thing, – and their operations so far had been sufficiently like the genuine article to impose upon the public in general, – if we except Champion and Coaldust, – even to the point of securing the assistance of the traffic-directing policeman.

But alas! with that one step further, which is so often fatal to great enterprises, they had sought to add a finishing touch of realism to their impersonation by the inclusion of a little feminine interest; and to that end Dilly had been added to the cast – or more likely had added herself – in the *role* of a young person of humble station bringing her affianced his tea.

And, not for the first time in the history of man, it was the woman who opened the door to disaster.

Dilly wore a natty print dress – probably my housemaid's – with a tartan shawl over her head. She had on her thickest shoes, but they were woefully smart and thin for a girl of her class. Moreover, her hair was beautifully arranged under the shawl, and her hands – though she had had the sense to discard her ruby and sapphire engagement-ring – were too white and her face was too clean to lend conviction to her impersonation. In short, in her desire to present a pleasing *tout ensemble* – an object in which I must say she had succeeded to perfection – Dilly had utterly neglected detail and histrionic accuracy.

Evidently she was not expecting a gallery. Two highly-interested concentric circles – one of people and one of dogs – round her *fiances* encampment was rather more than she had bargained for. She had emerged quite suddenly from a side street (which I knew led to a shortcut from home) and now paused irresolutely a few yards away, crimson to the roots of her hair, what time the errand-boy, with looks of undisguised admiration, continued to reiterate his desire to be pursued.

The crowd all turned and stared at poor Dilly. Obviously they did not know what to make of her. Possibly she was some one from the chorus of a musical comedy going to be photographed, possibly she was merely " a bit balmy," or possibly she was an advertisement for something, and would begin to distribute hand-bills presently. So far, she merely looked as if she wanted to cry.

It was Robin who saw her first. He immediately stepped over his newly-completed touch- line, and taking the spotted bundle and the tea-can from her hands, conducted her ceremoniously within the magic circle, saying, in a voice much more like his own than before –

" Come away, lassie !"

Dicky looked up from his labours at this, and beheld his *fiancee* for the first time. All he said was –

" By gad, you've done it after all! Bravo!"

But Dilly did not appear to be at all gratified.

She merely sat on Gerald's little mountain of paving-blocks, looking as if she could not decide whether to throw her apron over her face and scream, or take a header into the wigwam. My heart bled for her in spite of her folly. The crowd, deeply interested and breathing hard, stood round waiting for the performance to begin.

It was Coaldust who took the lead.

"Tip us a song and dance, Clara," he said encouragingly.

Robin, who had been making a show of unfastening the bundle, suddenly rose to his feet. Coaldust saw him.

"All right, Carnegie," he remarked hurriedly. " No offence, ole pal!"

But Robin turned to Dicky, and the two held a hasty conversation, whose nature I could guess. Dilly could not be exposed to this sort of thing any longer. They began to put on their coats.

"They are going to give it up," I said, not without . relief. " About time, isn't it ? Do you recognise them, Champion ? "

But Champion, I found, was gone – probably to establish an *alibi.* Perhaps he was right. Questions might be asked in the House about this.

When I turned again to the scene below I found that the crowd had thickened considerably, and that the policeman had once more left the traffic to congest itself, and joined in the game.

"You must tell that young woman to move on," he said to Dicky, not unkindly. "She's causin' a crowd to collect, and that's a thing she can be give in charge for."

"All right," said Dicky hurriedly, "we're all going."

The policeman, struck by this sudden anxiety to oblige, became suspicious.

" All of you ?" he said. " 'Ow about this mess in the road ?"

Robin came to the rescue.

" We'll be back presently and sort it," he said reassuringly.

"Of course," said Dicky, pulling himself together. " Back in 'arf a tick, governor!"

"Don't you go callin' me names," said the policeman, as the spectators indulged in happy laughter.

" Sorry ! – I mean, certainly!" said Dicky, getting flustered. (I could see Robin glowering at him.) "We are just going down the street a minute. This – er – girl has brought us a bitof bad news. There's been an accident happened, – er "

" To her puir old mither," put in Robin, whom I began to suspect of rather enjoying this entertainment for its own sake.

This heartrending piece of intelligence touched the crowd, and Coaldust was instantly forward in proposing an informal vote of condolence, which was seconded by a bare-armed lady in a deerstalker cap. But the policeman, evidently roused by our friends' ill-judged and precipitate attempt to strike camp, suddenly produced a pocket-book from his tunic, and said –

"It is my duty to take your names and addresses, together with the name of the firm employing you."

This announcement obviously disconcerted Dicky and Robin; for it is one thing to take part in a masquerade, and another to get out of the consequences thereof by cold-drawn lying.

However, the policeman was sucking his pencil and waiting, so Dicky said –

"You can get all the information you want from the Borough Surveyor."

It was a bold effort, but the policeman merely said –

" Your name, please I"

Dicky, fairly cornered, replied –

"Er – Samuel" – I thought at first he was going to say " Inglethwaite," and was prepared to drop a flower-pot on his head if he did; but he continued, with the air of one offering a real bargain at the price – " Phillipps."

" Two P's ? " inquired the constable.

" Three," said Dicky.

The policeman rolled a threatening eye upon him.

" Be careful!" he said in an awful voice.

"One of them comes at the beginning," said Dicky meekly.

"Haw, haw!" roared several people in the crowd, which was unfortunate for Dicky. He was one of those people who would risk a kingdom to raise a laugh.

"Address?" continued the policeman.

" Buck'nam Pallia!" shouted Coaldust, before any one else in the crowd could say it.

The policeman turned and directed upon him a look that would have entirely obfuscated a soberer man.

" I'll attend to you presently," he said in the exact tones which my dentist employs when he shuts me into the waiting-room. "Now then, your address? Come along!"

Dicky gave some address which I did not catch, and the representative of the law turned to Robin. The latter evidently saw rocks ahead if the inquisition was to be extended to the whole party. He said –

"Surely there is no need to take any more names."

" I'll be responsible for the lot," added Dicky eagerly – too eagerly. "Now let's be off! Come along Di – Liza!"

He took Dilly by the arm, and, preceded by Gerald, began to press through the crowd, which by this time extended almost right across the street.

But the now thoroughly aroused guardian of the peace, determined not to be rushed like this, broke away from Robin, who was engaging him in pleasant conversation, and, hastening after the retreating group, laid a detaining and imperious hand on Dilly's arm.

What happened next I was not quick enough to see. But there was a swirl and a heave in the crowd, and presently Dicky became visible, standing in a very heroic attitude with his arm round Dilly; while the policeman, with an awe- inspiring deliberateness which implied "Now you *have* gone and done it!" extricated himself majestically but painfully from the chasm in the road which had recently been occupying Dicky's attention, and into which Dicky in defence of his beloved had apparently pushed him.

Picking up his pocket-book and putting it back into his chest, and uttering the single and awful word " *Assault!"* the policeman produced a whistle and blew it.

Things were certainly getting serious, and I had just decided to send out the hotel porter to the policeman to tell him to bring his captives inside out of the way of the crowd, when I noticed that Robin was ploughing his way towards the outskirts of the throng, waving his arm as he went. Then I saw that his objective was another policeman – an Inspector this time. He was a gigantic creature, and Robin and he, slowly forging towards each other through the surrounding sea of faces, looked like two liners in a tideway.

Robin's conduct in deliberately attracting the notice of yet another representative of law and order appeared eccentric on the face of it, but his subsequent behaviour was more peculiar still.

He seized the newly-arrived giant by the arm, and drew him apart from the crowd, where he told him something which appeared to amuse them both considerably.

" Yewmorous dialogue," announced Coaldust to his neighbours, "between Cleop- artrer's Needle and the Moniment!"

But it was more than that, – it was deep calling to deep. Presently the explanation, or the joke, or whatever it was, came to an end, and the Inspector advanced threateningly upon the crowd.

" Pass along, there, pass along!" he cried with a devastating sweep of his arm. He spoke with a Highland accent, and I realised yet once more the ubiquity of that great Mutual Benefit Society which has its headquarters north of the Tweed.

The crowd politely receded about six inches, and through them, accompanied by Robin, the Inspector clove his way to the encampment, where Dicky, who seemed to be rapidly losing his head, was delivering a sort of recitative to every one in general, accompanied by the policeman on the whistle.

What the Inspector said to his subordinate I do not know, but the net result was that in a very short time the former was escorting the entire party of excavators down the street, attended by a retinue of small boys (who wereevidently determined to see if it was going to turn] out a hanging matter); while the latter, to whom the clearing of the "house" had evidently been deputed, set about that task with a vigour and ferocity which plainly indicated a well-meaning and zealous mind tingling under an entirely undeserved official snub.

They told me all about it in the smoking-room that night.

" The idea," began Dicky, " was "

" Whose idea was it ? " I inquired sternly.

"It was all of our idea," replied my future relative by marriage lucidly.

"But who worked it out?" I asked, – "the plot, the business, the ' props' ? It was a most elaborate production."

"Never you mind that, old man," said Dicky lightly. (But I saw that Robin was laboriously relighting his pipe and surrounding himself with an impenetrable cloud of smoke.) "Listen to the yarn. The idea was to stake out a claim in some fairly busy road and stay there for a given time – say, six o'clock till tea-time – and kid the passing citizens that we were duly authorised to get in the way and mess up the traffic generally. If we succeeded we weregoing to write to *The Times* or some such paper and tell what we had done – anonymously, of course – just to show how necessary Champion's Bill is."

" Have you written the letter ?"

"Yes."

" I wouldn't send it if I were you."

"Well, that's what Robin here has been saying."

"Putrid rot if we don't!" remarked Gerald, who had by this time washed his face, but ought to have been in bed for all that.

"We can't do it," said Robin. "For one thing, we have attracted quite enough public attention already, – it's bound to be in the papers anyhow, now, and that will probably give the Bill all the advertisement it needs, – and if we give the authorities any more clues our names may come out. For another thing, it wouldn't be fair to Hector MacPherson."

"Who is he?"

"That Inspector who came up at the critical moment. He was one of my first friends in London."

" I remember. Go on."

" I was thankful to see him, I can tell you. Well, he undertook to square that poor bewildered bobby, and to take steps to get the road cleared and the hole filled up."

"How?"

"There is a street being mended just round the corner, and he said he would get the foreman of the gang, who is a relation of his wife's, to send a couple of men to put things right immediately. It's probably done by now."

" Then I suppose we may regard the incident as closed."

" Yes, I suppose so."

There was a silence.

" It was a bit of a failure at the finish," said Dicky meditatively, "but it was a success on the whole – what?"

" Rather!" said his fellow-conspirators.

" Our chief difficulty," continued Dicky, " was to decide on the exact type of drama to present. I was all for our dressing up as foreigners, and relaying an asphalte street. It would have been top-hole to trot about in list slippers and pat the hot asphalte down with those things they use. And think of the make-up! – curly moustaches and earrings! And we could have jabbered spoof Italian. But then old Robin here, who I must say has a headpiece on him, pointed out that the scenery and props would be much too expensive. We should want a cart with a bonfire in it and a sort of witches' cauldron on top, and all kinds of sticky stuff; so we gave up that scheme. We did not feel inclined to mess with gas-pipes or electric wires either, in case we burst ourselves up; so we finally decided to select some street with a wooden pavement, and maul it about generally for as long as we could. If we got interfered with by anybody official, we meant to talk some rot about the Borough Surveyor, and skedaddle if necessary. But it all worked beautifully I"

" Where did you get your tools and tent ? "

" Robin managed that," said Dicky admiringly.

Robin looked extremely dour, and I refrained from further inquiry.

"Robin's got some rum pals, I *don't* think!" observed Gerald pertinently.

" Didn't I make these chaps up well ?" continued Dicky enthusiastically. " We roared when you passed us at breakfast-time without spotting us."

"Very creditable impersonation," I replied, getting up and knocking my pipe out. "I only hope I shan't have to resign my seat over it. If I may venture to offer a criticism, the weak spot in the enterprise was the idea of inviting your lady friends to come and take tea with you."

" Just what I said all along, my boy," remarked the experienced Gerald, wagging his head sagely. "That was what mucked up the show. Wherever there's a petticoat there's trouble. Oh, I *warned* them!"

On my way up to bed I flushed Dilly from a window-seat on the staircase, where she had evidently been lingering on the off- chance of a supplementary good-night from Dicky.

" Well? " I said severely.

"Well?"

" Do you know what time it is ? "

" I expect your wife will tell you that when you get upstairs," said Dilly.

I tried a fresh line.

"After the labours of to-day, I should have thought you would have been glad to go to bed," I said. "You imp!" And I laughed. There is something very disarming about the Twins' misdemeanours.

We turned and walked upstairs together, and paused outside Dilly's door.

" Good-night, Dilly," I said. " I admired your pluck."

"It wasn't me," said Dilly, in a very small voice.

"Not you?"

"N-no. I said I would come, because Dicky said I daren't, and at the last moment I funked it. (Adrian, I simply couldn't!) So Dolly went instead."

" Then that was Dolly all the time ? "

"Yes."

" And she went, just to – to "

" To save my face. She's a brick," said Dilly.

This, by the way, was the first occasion on which I realised the truth of Robin's dictum that Dilly and Dolly were girls of widely different character.

" And didn't the others recognise her ? "

" No. That's the best of it 1"

"Not Dicky?"

"No."

"Not even Robin? He is pretty hard to deceive, you know."

"No, not even Robin. *None* of them know, Good-night!"

But she was wrong.

5

SECTION 5

147
CHAPTER NINE.
THE POLICY OF THE CLOSED DOOR.

Dilly's wedding took place the following summer, just before Parliament rose, and the resources of our establishment were strained to the uttermost to give her a fitting send-off.

It is true that a noble relative, the head of my wife's family, offered his house for the reception, but Dilly emphatically declined to be married from any but mine, saying prettily that she would not leave the roof under which she had lived so happily until the last possible moment.

Accordingly we made immense preparations. The drawing-room on the first floor, accustomed though it was to accommodate congested and half-stifled throngs of human beings, was deemed too small for the mob of wedding-guests whom Kitty expected.

"You see, dear," she explained, "we cansquash up *good* people as much as we like, because their clothes don't matter; but women in wedding-frocks will be furious if they don't get enough elbow-room to show themselves."

Accordingly a marquee was erected in the garden at the back of the house, opening into the dining-room through the French windows, and it was arranged that Dicky and Dilly were to take their stand in the middle of the same, what time the guests, having lubricated their utterance at the *buffet* in the dining-room *en route,* filed past and delivered their congratulations. After that the company was to overflow into the garden, there to be moved by a concord of sweet sounds emanating from a band of assassins in pseudo-Hungarian uniforms.

"And if it rains," concluded Kitty desperately, "they must have an overflow meeting in the basement – that's all!"

My library, as I had feared, was appropriated for the presents, and for several days I transacted the business of State at the wash-handstand in my dressing-room, while a stream of callers, ranging from the members of a Working Men's Club in which Dilly was fitfully interested, down to an organisation of Kitty's whose exact title I can never recall (but which Dicky, onfirst seeing them, immediately summed up as "The Hundred Worst Women"), filed solemnly past rows of filigree coffee-services, silver-backed hair-brushes, and art pen-wipers.

Of the bride-elect I saw little, and when I did, she was usually standing, in a state of considerable *deshabille,* amid a kneeling group of myrmidons, who, with mouths filled with pins and brows seamed with anxiety, were remorselessly building her into some edifice of shimmering silk and filmy lace, oblivious of their victim's plaintive intimations that she was fit to drop.

Dicky invited Robin to be his best man, a proceeding which, while it roused some surprise among those who were expecting him to fix upon a friend of longer standing and greater distinction, showed his good sense, for my secretary proved himself a model of organisation and helpfulness. Although born and reared up in the straitest sect of some Scottish denomination, about which I am unable to particularise beyond the fact that they regarded the use of harmoniums in churches as " the worship of men's feet," he betrayed a surprising knowledge of Anglican ritual and stage effect.

On the wedding morning, having left thebridegroom securely tucked up in bed, under strict orders not to get up till he was called, Robin personally conducted a select party of those interested – Dolly, Dilly, another bridesmaid, and myself – to the church, where he showed us the exact positions of our entrances and exits; and then proceeded, with the assistance of Dolly, to plant hassocks about the chancel in such a manner as to leave us no doubts as to the whereabouts of our moorings (or "stances," as he called them) at the actual ceremony.

The party was reinforced at this point by the arrival of no less a person than the bridegroom, who, having risen from his slumbers in defiance of Robin's injunctions, was now proceeding to infringe the laws of propriety by coming in search of his beloved four hours before he was entitled to do so.

However, as Dilly rather pessimistically pointed out, it was probably the last time she would ever get a kind word out of him, so we gave them ten minutes together in the porch, while Robin interviewed vergers and Dolly intimidated perspiring persons with red carpets and evergreens.

On our return home Dilly was snatched awayby a cloud of attendant sprites, and we saw her no more until the time came for me to drive her to the church. We heard of her, though; for as we sat at luncheon, plying the bridegroom (who had collapsed after the complete and inevitable fashion of his kind about twelve o'clock) with raw brandy, a message came down from the upper regions, to the effect that Miss Dilly would take a couple of veal cutlets and a glass of Burgundy, as she wasn't going to be a pale bride if she could help it!

However, this half-hysterical gaiety came to an end in the face of reality, and in the carriage on the way to church poor Dilly wept unrestrainedly on my shoulder. I mopped her up to the best of my ability, but she was still sobbing when we reached the church door, to find the six bridesmaids, together with Phillis (inordinately proud of her office of train-bearer), preening themselves in the porch.

It had been arranged that the organ should break into "The March of the Priests," from 'Athalie' – Dicky's petition in favour of an ecclesiastical rendering of "The Eton Boating Song" had been thrown out with ignominy – as the bridal procession entered the nave. Unfortunately the organ-loft was out of sight of the west door, by which we were to enter, and the conveyance of the starting-signal to the proper quarter at exactly the right moment was a matter of some difficulty. However, Robin's gift for stage-management was sufficient to meet the emergency. When all was ready Dolly calmly mounting the steps of the font to an eminence which commanded a precarious but sufficient view of the body of the church, briefly fluttered a scrap of lace handkerchief, and then stepped demurely down into her place at the head of the bridesmaids. Simultaneously the organ burst into the opening strains of Mendelsohn's march – I suppose Robin had been waiting at some point of vantage to pass the signal on – and we advanced up the aisle, amid a general turning of heads and flutter of excitement.

The church was packed. In the back pew I remember noticing three young men with pads of flimsy paper and well-sucked pencils. I distinctly caught sight of the words "Sacred edifice" in the nearest MS., and I have no doubt the others contained it as well.

But Dilly was still quaking on my arm, and the only other spectacle which attracted my attention on the way up the aisle was that of my wife (looking very like a bride herself, I thought), sitting in a front pew with Master Gerald, that infant phenomenon shining re- splendently in a white waistcoat and a " buttonhole " which almost entirely obscured his features. Then I caught sight of Robin's towering shoulders and the pale face and glassy eye of the bridegroom, and I knew that we had brought our horses to the water at last, and all that now remained to do was to make them drink.

The rest of the ceremony passed off with due impressiveness, if we except a slight *contretemps* arising from the behaviour of my daughter, who, suddenly remembering that the junior bridesmaid but one had not yet passed any opinion on her new shoes, suddenly sat down on the bride's train, and, thrusting the shoes into unmaidenly prominence, audibly invited that giggling damsel's approbation of the same. However, the ever - ready organ drowned her utterance with a timely Amen, and Dicky and Dilly completed the plighting of their troth with becoming shyness but obvious sincerity.

Then came the inevitable orgy of osculation in the vestry, from which I escaped with nothing worse, so to speak, than a few scratches, despite an unprovoked and unexpected flank attack (when I was signing the register) from an elderly female in bugles, whom I at first took to be a rather giddy pew-opener, but who ultimately proved to be a maiden aunt of the bridegroom's.

After Dicky and Dilly – the latter miraculously restored to high spirits and looking radiant – had passed smiling and blushing down the aisle, to be received outside with breathless stares by a large assemblage of that peculiar class of people – chiefly females of a certain age – who seem to spend their lives in attending the weddings of total strangers, we all got home, where there was much champagne, and cake-cutting, and bride-kissing, and melody from the aforementioned musicians in the garden.

The presents – guarded with an air of studied aloofness by a wooden-jointed detective, clad in garments of such festal splendour as to delude several short - sighted old gentlemen into an impression that he was the bridegroom – played their usual invaluable part in promoting circulation among the guests, and supplying a topic for conversation. They certainly sparkled and glittered bravely in the library, where the blinds were drawn and the electric lamps turned on. (Kitty had seen to that. Silver looks so well by artificial light, and so, by a happy and unpremeditated coincidence, does the female sex.)

The bride and bridegroom departed at last, amid a shower of rice, with that emblem of conjugal felicity, the satin slipper, firmly adhering to the back of the brougham. (Master Gerald had seen to *that.*) Then the guests began to make their adieux and melt away, and presently we found ourselves alone in the marquee, a prey to that swift and penetrating melancholy that descends upon those who begin to be festive too early in the day, and find themselves unable to keep it up till bed-time.

However, there was a recrudescence of activity and brightness in the evening, as the idea of a small dance had been proposed and carried, and the invitations issued and accepted, during the five minutes which witnessed the departure of the more intimate section of the guests.

When I returned from the House about midnight -r-1 had gone there chiefly to dine, as lobster claws and melted ices appeared to be the only fare in prospect at home – tired to death, and conscious of an incipient cold in the head, arising from forced residence in a house in which hardly a door had been on its binges for three days, I became aware that I was once again the lessee of a cave of harmony.

The pseudo-Hungarian assassins were pounding out the latest waltz, with a disre-gard for time and tune which I at first attributed to champagne, but which a closer survey proved to be due to the fact that the band was being conducted, surprising as it may seem, by my brother-in-law, who had kindly undertaken to wield the *baton,* while the Chief Tormentor (or whatever his proper title may have been) charged him-self anew at the refreshment counter. A popping of corks in the supper- room apprised me of the fact that my guests were doing their best, at my expense, to make the Excise Returns a more cheerful feature of next year's Budget.

I went upstairs in search of a white waistcoat and one or two other necessary contributions to the festivity of the evening, picking my way with the utmost care among the greatly - engrossed couples who impeded every step; and finally arrived at my dressing-room, to find that that hallowed apartment had been turned into a ladies' cloak-room, and that every available article of furniture stood elbow-deep under some attractive combination of furs and feathers

I unearthed the things I required, but lacked the courage to stay and put them on. At anymoment I might be invaded by a damsel who had met with some mishap in the heat of the fray, and was now desirous, as they say in the navy, of " executing repairs while under steam." I accordingly left the room and mounted towards the top of the house. I had in my mind's eye a snug little apartment, situated somewhere in the attics, devoted chiefly to dressmaking operations, where I knew there was a mirror, and I might complete my toilet in peace.

With becoming modesty I penetrated to this haven by the back-stairs. I had just reached the top, which was opposite the door in question, when I heard voices. Evidently some one was coming up to this same landing by the front stair.

A man does not look his best when found creeping up his own back-stairs with a white waistcoat in one hand and a pair of pumps in the other, and I confess I retreated downwards and backwards a couple of paces. The stair on which I stood was unlighted, and I had a good view of the landing.

The voices came nearer, and I could now hear the rustling of silks and laces. Presently I recognised the voices, and immediately after this their owners came into view, with their backs almost towards me.

"This is the room I mean," said the man, indicating my goal.

"That! All right! Only I don't see why you should drag me all the way up here," said the girl. "There are much nicer sitting-out places downstairs. Still, anything for a rest. Come on!"

She entered the room, followed by her partner. I saw his broad back for a moment as it filled the doorway. Then he turned in my direction with his hand on the handle, and it seemed to me that he hesitated a moment.

Finally he shut the door firmly, and – I distinctly heard the key turned in the lock.

I went downstairs again.

It was four o'clock in the morning. The last guest had gone, the domestics had retired to their subterranean retreat, and the musicians had all been booked through to Saffron Hill in one cab.

The dawn was just breaking over the housetops on the other side of the square, and the sky was bathed in a curious heather-coloured light – a sure sign of a wet day to come, said hill-bred Robin. We stood out on the steps, – Kitty, Dolly, Robin, and I, – and Kitty put her arm round her sister's waist. I knew she was thinking of the absent Dilly.

Behind us, in the hall, Master Gerald, completely surfeited with about sixteen crowded hours of glorious life, lay fast asleep on a settee.

I looked curiously at Dolly as she leaned on her sister's shoulder. She was half a head taller than Kitty, and as she stood there, rosily flushed, in the dawn of her splendid womanhood, she might have stood for the very goddess whose first rays were now falling on her upturned face and glinting hair.

Then I looked at Robin, towering beside her, and suddenly I felt a little ashamed of myself.

For to tell the truth I had been very unhappy that evening, and I had been looking forward in a few minutes' time to unburdening myself to Kitty about recent events. But as I surveyed Dolly and Robin, curiously alike in their upright carriage and steady gaze, I suddenly realised that such a pair could safely be trusted to steer their own course; and I decided there and then not to communicate even to Kitty – my wife and Dolly's sister – the knowledge of what I had seen that night.

Kitty turned impulsively to her sister.

" After all, I've still got *you*, Dolly," she said.

I took a furtive glance at Robin's inscrutable countenance.

" I – *wonder!"* I said to myself.

" What, dear ? " said Kitty.

"Nothing. I must carry this young ruffian up to bed, I suppose."

Curiosity has been most unfairly ear-marked as the exclusive monopoly of the female sex. But as I stumbled upstairs that night, bearing in my arms the limp but stertorous carcase of my esteemed relative by marriage, I could not help wondering (despite my efforts to put away from me a matter which I had decided was not my business) exactly what Robin *had* said to Dolly behind that locked door.

CHAPTER TEN.

Robin's Way Of Doing It.

What happened when Robin locked the door on himself and Dolly is now set down here. Strictly speaking it ought to come later, but there is no need to make a mystery about it. I have taken the account of the proceedings mainly from the letter which Dolly wrote to Dilly three days later.

It would be useless to reproduce that document in full. In the first place, it contains a good deal that is not only irrelevant but absolutely incomprehensible. There is one mysterious passage, for instance, occurring right in the middle of the letter, beginning, *To turn the heel, knit to three beyond the seam-stitch, knit two together, purl one, turn: then knit ten, knit two together, knit one, purl one . . .* introduced by an airy, "By the way, dear, before I

forget" which appears to have no bearing
on the context whatever.

In the second place, Dolly's literary style is as breathlessly devoid of punctuation as that of most of her sex. Commas and notes of interrogation form her chief stock-in-trade, though underlining is freely employed. There is not a single full-stop from start to finish. The extracts from the letter here reproduced have been edited by me. Other details of the incident have been tactfully extracted by Kitty and myself – chiefly Kitty, I must confess – from the principals themselves, and the whole is now offered to the public, unabridged, with marginal comments, for the first tune.

On entering the little room on the landing Dolly dropped on to a shabby but comfortable old sofa behind the door, and said, with a contented sigh –

" I'm so tired, Robin. Aren't you ? Let's sit down and not talk till it's time to go downstairs again. It's – Robin, what *are* you doing ? "

Robin was locking the door.

That operation completed, he turned and looked round the little room. There was an arm-chair in the corner, but he came and sat down onthe sofa beside Dolly. Dolly gazed at him dumbly.

" He looked so utterly grim and determined " [says the letter], "that my heart began to bump in a perfectly fatuous way. I felt like a woman who is going to be murdered in a railway tunnel

" He sat down, and one of his huge hands was suddenly stretched towards me, and I thought at first he was trying to grab one of mine. I did my best to edge away along the sofa, but I was up against the end already.

" Then his hand opened, and something dropped into my lap. It was the key of the door.

"'I have locked it,' he said, 'not with any intention of keeping you in, but in the hope of keeping other people out. You are perfectly free to get up and go whenever you please, if you don't wish to listen to what I have to say.'

" Well, dear, I suppose I ought to have risen to my full height, and, with a few superb gestures of haughty contempt, have swept majestically from the room. But – I didn't! I saw I was in for another proposal, and as the man couldn't eat me I decided to let him do his worst.

" It was a weird proposal, though." *[Spelt' wierd.']* " It wasn't exactly what he said, because one is never surprised at anything a man may say when he is proposing; but the way he said it. All men say pretty much the same thing in the end, but most of them are so *horribly* nervous that they simply don't know what they're talking about for the first five minutes or so. (Do you remember poor little Algy Brock? He was nearly *crying* all the time. At least he was with me, and I suppose he waswith you too.) But Robin might have been having a chat with his solicitor the way he behaved. I'll tell you . . ."

Robin apparently began by telling Dolly, quite simply and plainly, that he loved her. Then he gave a brief outline of the history of his affection. It had begun at the very beginning of things, he said, almost as soon as he discovered that he could distinguish Dolly from Dilly without the aid of the brown spot. " And that was after I had been in the house just three days," he added.

For some time, it appeared, he had been content to be pleasantly in love. He enjoyed Dolly's society when it came his way, but with native caution he had taken care to avoid seeking too much of it in case he should gradually find himself unable to do without it.

" I saw from the first," he said, " that you were entirely unconscious of my feelings towards you; and I would not have had it otherwise. If I was to succeed at all it must be as an acquired taste; and acquired tastes, as you know, are best formed unconsciously."

Dolly nodded to show her detached appreciation of the soundness of this point.

"I permitted myself one indulgence," Robin continued. "I dedicated a book to you."

" 0-oh !" said Dolly, genuinely interested. "Was that me? Dilly and I thought it must be a girl in Scotland."

Then she realised that this was a step down from her pedestal of aloofness, and was silent again. Robin went on –

" Yes, it was you. It was a sentimental thing to do, but it afforded me immense pleasure. Love lives more on the homage it pays than that which it receives. Have you noticed that?"

"I have never thought about it," said Dolly distantly.

" I thought not," replied Robin; " because it shows, what I have always been tolerably certain of, that you have never been in love. However, to resume." [" *Like a lecture on Greek Roots, or something equally fusty"* observes Dolly at this point.]

"The time came, as it was bound to come, when I realised that I must tell you I loved you"

"I rather like the way he always said *'love'* straight out," comments Dolly: " most men are so frightened of it. They say 'am fond of,1 or 'care for,' or something feeble like that. All except the curate with pink eyes. (You remember him ? Dora Claverton took him afterwards on the rebound.) He said ' esteem highly,' I think."

"or leave this house altogether. But

before doing that I had to decide two things: firstly, whether I was good enough for you, and secondly, if not now, whether I ever should be."

Dolly's half-closed eyes opened a trifle wider. This was certainly a methodically-minded young man.

" It was difficult to decide the first question in practice," continued Robin. " In theory, of course, any man who is a *man* – honest, clean, and kind – is a fitting mate for any woman. Don't you think so ? "

"No," said Dolly.

"I see," said Robin gently. "The theoretical is mainly the man's point of view: woman looks straight to practical results. She is rather inclined to take the virtues I have mentioned for granted, or do without them; and she founds her opinion of a man almost solely upon his capacity for boring" her or stimulating her. In other words, she is guided by her instinct. Isn't she ? "

"Is she?" said Dolly, determined this time to maintain her attitude of indifference.

" I think so," said Robin. " However, knowing how impossible it is for one sex to look at a matter from the point of view of another, I decided to stick to my own methods. So Imade a summary of my points, good and bad. They are these: I am strong and healthy; I possess an appetite for hard work; I was born with brains; I have considerable capacity for organisation "

"Some people have a good conceit of themselves !" said Dolly.

"Every one should have," replied Robin with conviction. "And," he added, "most of us have. *I* have – *you* have!"

" Oh !" said Dolly indignantly.

" But a man may have a good conceit of himself," Robin continued soothingly, " without being what the world calls conceited. Modesty consists not in taking a low estimate of one's own worth, but in refraining from the expectation that the world will take a high one."

Dolly nodded gravely.

"I see," she said. "I didn't know you meant that. Yes, there is something in what you say."

" I thank you," said Robin. " It is very helpful to me to get this courteous hearing from you; for to tell you the truth," he added rather explosively, " I find it a very, very great effort to speak to you like this at all. You see, I am talking of things that go right to the centre of the human heart – things that a man neverspeaks of to a man, and only once to a woman. It has to be done, but it is hard, hard!"

He drew a long breath, in a manner which made the sofa tremble; and Dolly suddenly realised the height and depth of the barrier of reserve and pride that this grave and undemonstrative man had had to break down before he could offer her the view of his inmost soul to which he considered that she was entitled. She felt a sudden pang of awe, mingled with compassionate sympathy. She was not given to wearing her heart on her sleeve herself.

" Well," continued Robin, evidently relieved by this little confession, " those are my assets. On the other hand, I have no money, no position – I will not say no birth, for I come of good, honest stock – and my prospects are at present in the clouds. But to one type of wife all that would not matter a scrap. There are two types, you know – two types of *good* wife, that is."

"I would have given worlds," says Dolly here, "just to have said ' Oh !' or something; but for the life of me I couldn't help asking what the two types were."

"The first," said Robin, "is the wife wholoves her husband because she is proud of him, because he is successful and powerful, and people admire him; and not because she has any conception of or sympathy with the qualities which have made him what he is. To such a one the husband must come with his reputation ready made, and they will enjoy it together. The other type loves her husband because she sees through him, yet believes in him and sympathises with his aims, and intends to make a success of him. And she usually does."

" And which am I ?" inquired Dolly.

" The latter, undoubtedly – the higher type. And therefore, if there had been nothing else in the way, I think I should have given myself the benefit of the doubt. But M

"He turned and looked at me here," writes Dolly, and said –

"' But your feminine instinct is chafing against all this laborious weighing of pros and cons. In your own mind you summed up the situation ten minutes ago. I am – "impossible." Isn't that it?'

"My *dear,* I nearly *screamed,* for of course that is just what was in my mind. But I couldn't very well say so, so I just sat there and looked rather idiotic, and he went on –

"' In other words, I am not quite a gentleman.'

"Then I said quite suddenly –

"'Robin, whatever else you may be, you *are* a gentleman.'

"He got quite pink. 'Thank you,' he said. 'But for all that, I am too rough a suitor for such a polished little aristocrat as yourself.' (Rather cheek, that! After all, Dilly, we're five feet seven.) ' We live in an artificial sort of world; and a man, in order not to jar on those around him, requires certain social accomplishments. I have few – at present. You have taught me a great deal, but I should still rather discredit you as a husband. My want of polish would 'affront' you, as we say in Scotland. I am a better beater than shot; I can break a horse better than I can ride it; and I dance a reel better than I waltz. I have strength, but no grace; ability, but no distinction. Of course, if you and I really loved each other – you being of Type Two – none of these things would matter. But for all that, it would hurt you to see people smiling at your husband's little *gaucheries,* wouldn't it?'

" I didn't answer, and he got up and went and leaned against the mantelpiece.

"' Listen,' he said,' and I will tell you what I have decided to do. I have made up my mind not to have a try for you – badly though I want it – till I consider that I have reached your standard. I fixed that standard myself, so it is a very, very high one. I have been schooling myself and shaping myself to attain it ever since I met you. But I have not quite reached it yet, and therefore I have nothing to ask of you now.'"

"Then what on earth have you brought me here for ?" inquired Dolly, feeling vaguely aggrieved.

Robin surveyed her rather wistfully, and then smiled in a disarming fashion.

"That was weakness," he said, "sheer weakness. But I think it was pardonable. I saw, now that your sister was married, that the days of your old irresponsible flirtations were over, and that you would henceforth regard proposals of marriage as much more serious things than hitherto. Consequently you might marry any day, without ever knowing that a little later on you would have received an offer from me. I have brought you here, then, to tell you that I am a prospective candidate, but that I do not feel qualified to put down my name at present. Ideally speaking, I ought to have kept silence until the moment when I considered that I was ready for you; but – well, there are limits to self-repression, and I have allowed myself this one little outbreak. All I ask, then, is that in considering other offers you will bear somewhere in the back of your mind the remembrance that you will, if you desire it, one day have the refusal of me. I admit that the possibility of your being influenced by the recollection Is very remote, but I am going to leave nothing undone that *can* be done to get you."

" By this time," Dolly continues elegantly, " I was getting considerably flummoxed. The whole business was very absurd and uncomfortable, but I couldn't help feeling rather complimented at the way he evidently regarded me – as a sort of little tin goddess on a pedestal out of reach, being asked to be so good as to stand still a moment while Eobin went to hunt for the steps – and I also felt a little bit afraid of him. He was so quiet and determined over it all. He seemed to have it all mapped out in a kind of time-table inside him. However, I pulled myself together and decided to contribute my share to the conversation. I hadn't had much of a look in, so far.

" So I settled down to talk to him like a mother. I began by saying that I was very much obliged and honoured, and all that, but that he had better put the idea out of his head once and for all. I liked him very much, and had always regarded him as a great friend, quite one of the family – you know the sort of stuff – but

" It was no good. He held up his hand like a policeman at a crossing, and said –

"'Please say nothing. I have asked you no question of any kind, so no answer is required. All that I have said to-night has been in the nature of an *intimation*.' (0-h! how like church!)

" Then he sat down on the sofa beside me, very gently, and said –

"'The intimation in brief is this. I love you; and some day, please God, I shall ask you to many me. But not until I feel that you would lose *nothing* by doing so.'

"We both sat very still for a few minutes after that I fancy we were both doing a little thinking. My chief reflection was that Robin had had rather the better of the interview, because he had made me listen to him when I was determined not to. Suddenly Bobin said –

"'Now that the business part of this conversation is over, I am going to allow myself a luxury. I have been talking most of the time about myself. For just five minutes I shall talk about you. I will tell you what I think of you.'

" He looked at his watch and began. Dilly, I had no idea I had so many good points! He put them better than any man has ever done before. But then the other men were always so jumbled up, and this creature was as cool and collected as if he were reading a Stores Catalogue.

" But he let himself go at last. It was my fault, though. I was in rather a twitter by this time, for although the whole thing was simply absurd – of course one couldn't marry a wild untamed creature like that, *could* one, Dilly ? – I couldn't help seeing what a *man* he was, and feeling sorry that things couldn't have been a bit different, if only for his sake. So I gave him my hand" [I can see her do it] "and said: 'Poor old Bobin!'

"He *seized* it – my child, it has waggled like a blancmange ever since t – and kissed it. Then, quite suddenly, he broke out into a sort of rhapsody – like ' *The Song of Solomon'* only nicer – with his head bowed over my hands. (He had got hold of the other one too, by this time.) I felt perfectly helpless, so I let him run on. I shan't tell you what he said, dear, hecause it wouldn't he cricket. Anyhow, a perfectly idiotic tear suddenly rolled down my nose – after all, I had had a *fearfully* long day – and I tried to pull my hands away. Eobin let them go at once.

"' You are right. The time for such things is not yet,' he said, in a queer Biblical sort of way. ' It was a sudden weakness on my part. I had not meant it, you may be sure.'

"The only thing I *am,* sure about," I said, feeling thoroughly vexed about the tear, "is that we have been in this room nearly an hour. Please unlock the door.

" Then we went downstairs."

After that follow one or two postscripts of a reflective nature, the general trend of which seems to indicate that Robin is rather a dear, but quite impossible.

"A flippant and unfeeling letter," you say, sir ? Perhaps. But, there is often no reserve so deep or so delicate as that which is veiled by a frivolous exterior and a mocking attitude towards sentiment in general Some sensitive people are so afraid of having their hearts dragged to light that, to escape inquisition, they pretend they do not possess any. Moreover, I know Dolly well enough to be certain that she was not quite so brutally unkind to Eobinduring this interview as she would have us believe.

" The blundering creature ! He went about it in *quite* the wrong way," you say, madam? Very likely. But if a woman only took a man when he went about it in exactly the right way, how very few marriages there would be!

BOOK TWO.
THE FINISHED ARTICLE.
CHAPTER ELEVEN.
A MISFIRE.

There is an undefinable character and dis- tinctiveness about Sunday morning which is not possessed by any other day of the week.

Not that the remaining six are lacking in individuality. Monday is a depressed and reluctant individual; Tuesday is a full-blooded and energetic citizen; Wednesday a cheerful and contented gentleman who does not intend to overwork himself to-day, – this is probably due to the fact that we used to have a half- holiday on Wednesdays at school; and when I got into Parliament *I* found that the same rule held there; Thursday

I regard as one who ploughs steadily on his way, lacking enthusiasm but comfortably conscious of a second wind; Friday is a debilitated but hopeful toiler, whose sole joy in his work lies in anticipating its speedy conclusion; and Saturday is a radiant fellow with a straw hat and a week-end bag.

Still, one week-day is very like another at waking time. My mental vision, never pellucid, is in its most opaque condition in the early grey of the morning; and at Oxford, I remember, I found it necessary to instruct my scout to rouse me from slumber in some such fashion as this : " Eight o'clock on Thursday mornin', sir!" (as if I had slept since Monday at least), or " 'Alf - past nine, slight rain, and a Toosday, sir!"

However, no one was ever yet needed to inform me that it was Sunday morning. This is perhaps natural enough in town, where the silence of the streets and the sound of bells proclaim the day; but why the same phenomenon should occur in the middle of a Highland moor, where every day is one glorious open-air Sabbath, passes my comprehension.

I discussed the problem after breakfast as I sat and smoked my pipe in the heathery garden of Strathmyrtle, a shooting - lodge at which we were being hospitably entertained by Kitty's uncle, Sir John Rubislaw, a retiredAdmiral of the Fleet, whose forty years' official connection with Britannia's realm betrayed itself in a nautical roll, syncopated by gout, and what I may describe as a hurricane-deck voice. My three companions in the debate were my host, Master Gerald, and another guest in the house, one Dermott, an officer in a Highland regiment.

The Admiral ascribed my Sabbath intuition to the working of some inward and automatic monitor; while Dermott, among whose many sterling qualities delicate fancy was not included, put it down to the smell of some special dish indigenous to Sunday breakfast. My brother-in-law's contribution to the debate was an unseemly and irreverent parallel between Saturday night potations and Sunday morning "heads."

To us entered Dolly and Phillis.

Our hostess, together with Kitty and the other girl of the party – an American young lady of considerable personal attractions – had driven off to church in what is locally called a "machine." The duties of escort had been voluntarily undertaken by an undergraduate named Standish, who was the latest recruit to the American young lady's army of worshippers. The rest of us had stayed at home – the Admiral because he not infrequently did so; I because I was expecting Robin back by the " machine" (which was to pick him up at a wayside station, where he had been sitting on his portmanteau ever since six o'clock that morning, having been dropped there by the night mail from London), and was anticipating two or three hours' solid work with him; Gerald because he had succeeded in evading his eldest sister's eye during the search for church recruits; Dolly to look after Phillis; and Captain Dermott for reasons not unconnected with Dolly.

It was Phillis's birthday, but out of consideration for Scottish views on Sabbath observance the festivities in connection with that anniversary had been postponed until the morrow. However, this did not prevent my daughter from demanding (and obtaining) various special privileges of an unofficial character this hot Sunday morning. Consequently a spiritually willing but carnally incompetent band, consisting of one jovial but arthritic baronet, one docile but self-conscious warrior, one indulgent but overheated parent, and Dolly – Gerald stood scornfully aloof – were compelled todevote the next two hours to a series of games, stage-plays, and allegories of an innocuous but exhausting description.

We began by joining hands and walking in a circle, solemnly chanting a ditty of the "I-saw-a-ship-a-sailing" variety, which culminated in the following verse –

" Then three times round went that gallant ship,

Then three times round went she ;

Then three times round went that gallant ship –

(Here we were commanded by the mistress of the revels, in a hoarse and hurried stage whisper, to be ready to fall down)

– And sank to the bottom – of – the – sea!"

" Now all fall down !" screamed Phillis.

We did so, and lay on the grass in serried heaps. The remark which the Admiral made when my left elbow descended upon his gouti- est foot was fortunately obscured by the fact that his face was inside his hat at the moment.

After that we performed the "most lamentable comedy" of "The Three Bears." Phillis assigned the parts, reserving for herself the *rdle* of Curly Locks and Stage Manager. Dolly was cast for Mother Bear, Captain Dermott for Father Bear, and I for Baby Bear. TheAdmiral, at his own urgent request, was allotted the comparatively unimportant part of Baby Bear's bed, and sat nursing his foot and observing with keen relish the preparations of the Bear family for their morning walk. We set out at last, all three on our hands and knees, Dolly and Dermott crawling amicably side by side, heroically regardless of white skirt and Sunday sporran; I, as befitted my youth and station, bringing up the rear.

The Bears having vacated their domicile (the grass plot), Curly Locks, after much furtive peeping round bushes, entered and advanced to the rustic table, where she proceeded to test the contents of the various porridge-bowls (represented by two tobacco - pouches and an ash-tray respectively).

" Too hot!" she said, after sampling the first bowl.

" Too cold!" she continued, trying the next.

" A-a-ah!" she cried, coming to the third; and swallowed its contents (some heather-tops) with every appearance of enjoyment.

After that came the inspection of the beds (two sofa-cushions and the Admiral), and finally Curly Locks retired to rest on her grand- uncle's knee.

Then the Three Bears came painfully back from the shrubbery, and Curly Locks' acts of spoliation were revealed one by one. My assumption of grief on the discovery of my empty porridge-bowl was so realistic that the Stage Manager sat up in bed and commended me for it. Finally we went the round of the furniture; Curly Locks was duly discovered; and I was engaged in a life-and-death struggle for her shrieking person with the bed itself, when there was a crunching of gravel, and the "machine" drove up with Robin inside it.

After my secretary had greeted those of us whom he knew, and been interrupted in the middle of a rapturous embrace from Phillis to be introduced to those whom he did not, I took him off indoors for a meal, through the breakfast-room window, and opened the portfolio of correspondence which he had brought me from London.

"Hallo! Here is a letter for Dermott," I said. "I'll take it to him."

I stepped through the window and handed the letter to Dermott, who was falling into line for a fresh game just outside.

"That envelope looks terribly official," said Dolly. " What does it all mean ? "

"I expect it means Aldershot," said Dermott ruefully. " However, I shan't open it till lunch- time." And he stuffed the offending epistle into his pocket, and returned to the game in hand with a zest and abandon that betrayed ulterior motives in every antic.

We had seen a good deal of Captain Dermott that summer. Somehow he had been in nearly every house we had visited; and his laborious expressions of pleased surprise at meeting us there had now given way to specious and transparent explanations of his own presence. The experts at countless tea - tables and shooting- lunches were practically unanimous in the opinion that Dolly could land her fish when she chose now; and as the fish was a good fellow, and could offer her three thousand a-year and the reflected glory of a D. S. O., it was generally conceded that my youngest sister-in-law – have I ever mentioned that Dolly was the junior Twin ? – was about to do extremely well for herself.

I sat by Robin as he consumed his breakfast, and waded through my correspondence. There was a good deal to sign and a good deal to digest, and a good deal that was of no importance whatsoever. But the *clou* of the wholebudget was contained in a private letter from my Chief. I read it.

"My word, Robin!" I said. "There's to be a Dissolution in January."

There was no answer, and I looked up.

Robin was not listening. His attention had wandered to the game in progress on the lawn. This was one of Phillis' most cherished pastimes, and was called " Beckoning." The players, except the person who for the time being filled the *role* of " It," stood patiently in a row, until " It," after mature consideration, beckoned invitingly to one of them to approach. This invitation might or might not be a genuine one, for sometimes the player on responding was received by the beckoner with hisses and other symptoms of distaste, and fell back ignominiously on the main body. But if you were the *real* object of the beckoner's affections, you were greeted with embraces and a cry of " I choose you!" and succeeded to the proud post of " It."

It was a simple but embarrassing game, calling for the exercise of considerable tact when played by adults. At the present moment Phillis was beckoner, while Dolly, Dermotfc, and the Admiral stood meekly in line awaiting selection. Dolly an. d the Admiral were each called without being chosen, and Phillis's final selection proved to be Dermott, who, having received an enthusiastic salute from the retiring president, now stood sheepishly on one leg surveying the expectant trio before him.

He began by beckoning to his host; and, having relieved that gentleman's ap- prehensions by sibilant noises, waggled a nervous finger at Dolly. Dolly advanced obediently.

"Choose her, if you like," said Phillis magnanimously.

Dermott's martial eye kindled, but he made no sign, and the game faltered in its stride for a moment.

" Say," interpolated the prompter, " ' I choose you !' and then k "

But Dermott, hastily emitting a hiss which must have cost him a heartrending effort, relegated the greatly relieved Dolly to the ranks, and smoothed over the situation by "choosing" my daughter, to that young person's undisguised gratification.

It was at this phase in the proceedings that Robin's attention began to wander from the affairs of State, and I had to repeat my news of the impending Dissolution to him twice before he grasped its full significance. Even then he displayed about one-tenth of the excitement I should have expected of him; and finally he admitted that he was somewhat *derange* after his night journey, and suggested a postponement of business in favour of a little recreation on the lawn.

We accordingly added ourselves to the party, just in time to join the cast of Phillis' next production. This was an ambitious but complicated drama of an allegorical type, in which Robin appeared – not for the first time, evidently – as a boy called Henry, and Phillis doubled the parts of Henry's mother and a fairy. These two *roles* absorbed practically the whole of what is professionally known as "the fat" of the piece, and the other members of the company were relegated – to their ill-disguised relief – to parts of purely nominal importance.

The curtain rose (if I may use the expression) upon Henry's humble home, where Henry was discovered partaking of breakfast (fir-cones). He complained bitterly to his mother of the hardship of (a) early rising, (6) going to school, and (c) enduring chastisement when he got there. The next scene revealed him in class, where the schoolmaster (Dolly, assiduously prompted by Phillis) asked him a series of questions, which he answered so incorrectly as to incur the extreme penalty of "the muckle tawse." (Here what textual critics term "internal evidence of a later hand" peeped out unmistakably.) The punishment having been duly inflicted by Dolly with a rug-strap, Henry retired, suffused with tears, to "a mountain-top," where he gave vent to a series of bitter reflections on the hardness of his lot and the hollowness of life in general.

He must have "gagged" unduly here, for presently he was cut short by a stern admonition to "wish for a fairy."

"I wish for a fairy," said Henry dutifully.

Phillis, given her cue at last, pirouetted before him with outstretched skirts.

" Go on !" she whispered excitedly. " Say, ' I wish that all Pain was Pleasure and all Pleasure Pain.'"

" Oh, sorry !" said Henry. " I wish that all Pain was Pleasure and Pleasure Pain."

" Have then thy wish!" announced the fairy solemnly, and fluttered away.

The drama thereafter pursued a remorselessly logical and improving course. Having got his wish, the luckless Henry found that his only moments of pleasure were those during which he was enduring the tawse, getting out of bed on a cold morning, or doing something equally unpleasant. On the other hand, his comfortable bed had become so painful that he could only obtain rest by filling it with stones; and his matutinal porridge was only made palatable by the addition of a handful of gravel.

After a fruitless interview with the family physician (Captain Dermott), in which the patient's mother set forth her offspring's symptoms with embarrassing frankness, Henry was compelled, as a last resort, to pay one more visit to the mountain-top. The indulgent fairy kindly agreed to put things right, but only under penalty of an improving homily on contentment with one's lot and the fatuity of asking for what you do not really want. This was only half finished when the party returned from church, and Phillis, realising that the absolute despotism of the last few hours would now be watered down by an unsentimental mother into a limited monarchy at the best, retired within her shell and declared the revels at an end.

II.

"What was the church like?" I inquired at lunch.

"I have witnessed more snappy entertainments," remarked Miss Buncle, the American girl, through her pretty nose. " Still, we smiled some. Mr Standish here got quite delirious when the minister prayed for 'the adjacent country of England, which, as Thou knowest, O Lord, lies some twa hundred miles to the sooth of us,' – I'm sorry I can't talk Scotch, Mr Fordyce, – as if he was afraid that Providence might mail the blessing to the wrong address and Iceland would get it."

Kitty broke in upon Miss Buncle's reminiscences.

" Who do you think we saw in church ?" she said. "I nearly forgot to tell you. Your uncle, Robin – Sir James Fordyce !"

Robin nodded his head in a confirmatory way.

"He is often up here at this time of year," he said.

" He has friends here, perhaps ? " said I.

"Oh yes; he has friends."

I could tell from Robin's voice that he wasnursing some immense joke, but he betrayed no inclination to share it with us. Kitty went on.

" He was sitting in a pew with some farmery- looking people. There was a patriarchal old man, very stately and imposing, rather like – like "

" Moses ?" I suggested.

" No. I don't *think* Moses was like that."

I had got as far as ' Aar' – when Lady Rubislaw said –

"Elijah?"

" That's it," replied Kitty. " *Just* like Elijah." (All things considered, I cannot imagine why Moses would not have done as well.) "Then beside him was a perfectly dear old lady. Not so very old either; say sixty. Of course they may not have belonged to Sir James at all: he may just have been put in their pew. Still, they kept handing him Bibles, and looking up places for him at singing time."

"That means nothing," said L "It's the merest courtesy here."

"True," said our hostess. "I was having a most lovely little doze during the Second Lesson, or whatever they call it, when a most officious young woman three or four pews away took up an enormous Bible, found the place, squeaked down the aisle, and thrust it under my nose.

I had to hold it up for fifty-seven verses," she concluded pathetically.

" Did you go and speak to Sir James after the

I o *f*

service ?" I inquired.

" No. That was *this* child's fault," said Kitty, indicating Miss Buncle.

"How?"

"Well, there was a rather gorgeous-looking chieftain sort of person sitting in a front pew, and I saw Maimie twisting her head all during the service to look at him."

"Yes," admitted the culprit frankly. "Put me in the neighbourhood of a kilt, and I'm a common rubberneck straight away, Mr Ingle- thwaite. I'm just *mad* to know all those cunning tartans by heart."

" The moment the service was over," continued my wife severely, " I saw her edging through the crowd in the churchyard towards the chieftain. For a moment I thought she was going to ask him his name."

" I *wasn't!* " declared Miss Buncle indignantly.

"No, you did worse. She got close to the unfortunate man," continued my wife to us, " and suddenly I noticed that she had in her hand one of those little books you buy at railway bookstalls in the Highlands, with patterns of all thetartans in them and the name of the clan underneath. By the time I got up to her she had found the right tartan in the book, and was matching it up against the back of the poor unconscious creature's kilt. Then she turned to me in a triumphant sort of way and simply *bellowed* – ' M'Farlane!'"

"We shall probably be hauled up before the Kirk-session," said the Admiral. " But I wonder who Sir James Fordyce's friends can be. I know most of the people who have shootings about here, but none of them are friends of his that I can think of. We must get him to come and shoot here one day. Bather late for tomorrow's drive, but there will be another on Thursday. I wonder who his host is, though ? "

"I might help you," said Bobin. "An old man, you said, with his wife?"

"Yes – oldish," said Kitty.

"Was there a son with them?"

"N-no."

" No ? Well, he would be away at the lamb- sales, perhaps," said Bobin reflectively. "Was there a daughter?"

" Now you mention it," said Kitty, " there was. A nice, bonny-looking girl. Twenty-four, I should say."

" Twenty-three," said Robin.

We all turned on him.

"Now then, what is all the mystery? Out with it! Who is the girl – eh?"

" She would be my sister," said Robin calmly. " And the others were my father and mother."

There -vas a little gasp of surprise all round the table. Robin went on –

" My home is just seven miles from here. This is the first time I have got near my folk for six years. To-morrow I mean to go and see them. And they would like fine, I know," he added a little shyly, " if some of you would come with me."

"I'll come," said Kitty promptly. "I should love to meet your mother, Robin."

" May / come, Uncle Robin 1" piped Phillis. " For a birfday treat," she added, in extenuation.

Applications for an invitation rained in. Apart from a desire to please a man whom we all respected – and our ready offers undoubtedly did please him – I think we were all a little curic-us to view the mould which had turned Robin out.

"You can't *all* go," said the Admiral at last. "There's the grouse-drive to-morrow, and eight butts to fill; not to mention the need of female society at lunch."

Finally it was arranged that Robin should take Kitty and Phillis over on a sort of preliminary call, and they could arrange for the establishment of more substantial relations.

But that evening, as the ladies were having their candles lit at the foot of the staircase, I heard Robin say to Dolly –

"Will you come with us to-morrow?"

Dolly seemed to consider, and was about to reply, when Dermott, who never seemed very far away now, cut in.

" Too late, Fordyce! Miss Rubislaw has promised to come and load for me in my butt to-morrow afternoon."

"No, I'm afraid it can't be managed this time, Robin," said Dolly. "But I am coming with you later in the week, if you'll take me."

Robin said nothing.

Now Dolly, I knew, did not approve of the inclusion of females in the business part of a day's shooting; and she regarded Miss Buncle and her twenty-eight bore with pious horror. The fact that she had consented to come and hold Dermott's second gun to-morrow seemed to indicate that that gallant sportsman had accomplished a feat which had already proved too much for several highly deserving youngmen – I *was* not quite sure that Robin was not one of them; and there seemed to be every reason to anticipate (especially since he was due to start for Aldershot to-morrow night) that when the Captain returned from the chase to-morrow afternoon, his bag would include one head of game of an interesting and unusual variety. .

m.-

At ten o'clock next morning we met the keepers, dogs, and beaters not far from the first line of butts on the moor. There was a hot sun, and the bees were bumbling in the heather. Somehow Whitehall seemed a long way off.

The number of guns had been brought up to seven by the inclusion of a neighbouring laird – one Gilmerton of Nethercraigs – and his son.

"All the same, we are still a man short," complained the Admiral, to whom a house-party was a ship's company, and a day's shooting a sort of terrestrial naval manoeuvre. "However, we will cut out the end butt ineach drive and put a stop there to turn the birds farther in. Now we'll draw for places. Each man to take the butt whose number he draws, counting from the right and moving up one place after each drive. And Heaven help the man who draws number four now, for it means number seven and a climb up The Pimple for him directly after lunch ! "

There was a general laugh at this, which swelled to an unseemly roar when I drew the fatal number.

However, after lunch was a long way off, and I trotted contentedly to number four and settled down to a pipe, while the head-keeper led off his mixed multitude of assistants, dogs, boys, and red flags to make a *d&our* and work the game up towards us.

The first drive was simple. We were in a long and rather shallow glen, across which ran a low ridge, dividing it into two almost equal sections. The butts were placed along this ridge ; and after the birds had been sent over us the beaters would work round to the other end of the glen and drive them back again. The shooting would be easy, for the ground lay flat and open in either direction.

I found myself between Standish and Gerald ; the former on my right, and the latter, together with the young keeper to whom his shooting education had been entrusted, in the butt on my left. Beyond Standish was Der- mott, the crack shot of the party, and beyond Dermott, in number one butt, was the Admiral. The Gilmertons, *pbre et fils,* occupied the butts on the extreme left.

The drive was moderately successful. At first the birds came along singly, mostly on the right, and fell an easy prey to Dermott and the Admiral. But presently a great pack got up comparatively near the butts, and fairly "rushed" us. I brought off an easy right and left straight in front of me, and then, snapping out my cartridges and slipping another in, I swung round and just managed to bring down a third bird with a "stern chaser" – a feat which I regretted to observe no one else noticed, for there was a perfect fusilade all along the line at the moment. Master Gerald, who had discharged his first barrel straight into the " brown," succeeded, in obedience to his mentor's admonitions, in covering an old cock- grouse with his second, and carefully following that flustered fowl's course with the point of his gun, pulled the trigger just as it skimmed, low down, with an agitated squawk, between his butt and mine. I heard the shot rattle through the heather, and two pellets hit on my left boot.

The congenial task of telling Gerald, in a low but penetrating voice, exactly what I thought of him, occupied my attention so fully for the next minute that I failed to observe a blackcock which suddenly swung up into view and whizzed straight past my head, to the audible annoyance of the distant Admiral and the undisguised joy of my unrepentant relative.

No more birds came after that, and presently, the line of beaters having advanced within range, we put down our guns and collected the slain. We had not done badly, considering the fact that the main body of the birds had swerved away to our left over the unoccupied butt, despite the valiant efforts of an urchin with a red flag to turn them. Dermott headed the list with four and a half brace, and Gerald brought up the rear with a mangled corpse which had received the contents of his first barrel point - blank at a distance of about six feet. The laird of Nethercraigs (a cautious and economical sportsman, who was reputed never to loose off hisgun at anything which did not come and perch on his butt) had fired just three cartridges and killed just three birds, but his son had seven. The Admiral and Standish had also had average luck, and altogether we had fourteen and a half brace to show for our exertions.

OS went the beaters again, and we changed butts and waited. The second drive gave us fewer birds but better sport. There were no great packs, but we got plenty to do in the way of sharp-shooting, and Gerald's keeper – a singularly ambiguous title in this case – succeeded by increased vigilance in preserving me from being further sniped by my enterprising brother-in-law.

We totalled up twelve brace this time, and then made ready for a tramp to the next line of butts, away round the shoulder of a fairly distant hill.

" We may as well spread out and walk 'em up this bit," said our host. "We can't have the dogs, though, as the keepers and beaters are going a different way; and each man will have to carry what he shoots. In that case we'll leave rabbits alone. Gerald, you had better get to the extreme left of the line. That will limit the risk to one man!"

"I I I carry home your bag if you'll carry mine, Gerald," cried Standish facetiously, as my brother - in - law, a trifle offended at the Admiral's last pleasantry, proceeded with much dignity to his allotted place.

Gerald was almost out of earshot, but he waved a defiant acquiescence.

We tramped round the shoulder of the hill, keeping our distance as well as we could on the steep slope, and occasionally putting up something to shoot at. My bag this time made no great demands on my powers of porterage, consisting as it did of a solitary snipe. However, when nearly an hour later we gathered at the foot of the next line of butts – the last before lunch – most of us were carrying something. Standish gleefully displayed two hares and a brace of grouse.

"There is something for Master Gerald to carry back to the luncheon-cart," he said. " I wonder what he has got for me. Where is he ?"

"I don't quite know," said Dermott, who had been Gerald's nearest neighbour. "He was so oflended by our gibes about the danger of his society that he walked rather wide of me. He kept down at the very foot of the hill most of the time, almost out of sight."

"I hope he hasn't shot himself," said the Admiral rather anxiously.

" Never fear !" said I. "That will not be his end. Here he is."

Sure enough, Gerald appeared at this moment. He was empty-handed.

Simple and primitive jests greeted him.

" Hallo, old man, what have you shot – eh ? Where is your little lot ?"

Gerald smiled seraphically.

" You'll find it down there," he said – " in that patch of bracken, Standish. I left it for you to bring up. Rather heavy for me."

" What on earth have you shot ?" we cried involuntarily.

" A sheep," said Gerald calmly.

Great heavens!

We rushed down the hill as one man – and came up again looking not a little hot and uncommonly foolish. The sheep was there, it is true, stiff and stark in the bracken; but more senses than one apprised us of the fact that it had been dead for considerably more than five minutes. Gerald had stumbled on to the corpse, and had turned his discovery, we afterwards admitted, to remarkably good advantage. It was "Mr Standish's turn," as Miss Buncle, inthe picturesque but mysterious vernacular of her race, remarked at luncheon, " to hold the baby this time."

After the third drive we gladly put up our guns and tramped down the hillside to the road below, where the ladies were waiting and the feast was spread. After we had disposed of grouse sandwiches, whisky-and-water, and jammy scones, and were devoting our post - prandial leisure to repose or dalliance with the fair – according as we were married or single – Lady E/ubislaw inquired –

" Where are you shooting this afternoon, John?"

"The Neb, first," replied the Admiral. "And that reminds me, the man who drew the top butt had better start now, or he'll be late."

With many groans, and followed by the mingled derision and sympathy of the company, I picked up my *impedimenta* and started, leaving the others to decide who, if any, of the shooters was to have the honour of entertaining a lady in his butt.

The Neb was a great mountain spur, whose base ran to within two or three hundred yards of our resting-place. In appearance it roughly resembled a mighty Napoleonic nose. The buttsran right up the ridge of that organ; and nine hundred feet above where we sat, just below an excrescence locally known as " The Pimple," lay mine.

I reached my eyrie at last, and having laid my flask, tobacco-pouch, and twelve loose sart- ridges where I could reach them most handily on projecting shelves of peat inside the butt – I love neatness and method : Kitty says that when (if ever) I get to heaven I will decline to enter until I have wiped my boots, – settled down to enjoy a superb view and take note of the not altogether uninteresting manner in which the other members of the party were disposing themselves for the drive.

Just below me were Standish and Miss Buncle, the lady a conspicuous mark for all men (and grouse) to behold by reason of a red tarn o' shanter, the sight of which made me regret that its wearer was not employed as a beater. In the butt below were Dermott and Dolly – both very workmanlike and inconspicuous. Below them came the Admiral, with his wife (she always came and sat behind him, like a remarkably smart little powder-monkey, during the afternoon drive): below them, the Gilmertons; and last of all, thank Heaven! Gerald.

The shooting on this beat would not be easy, though birds were always plentiful. They came round the face of the hill at very short range and express speed. My particular butt was notoriously difficult to score from. There was an awkward hummock in front of it, and driven birds swinging into view round this were practically right over the butt before its occupant could get his gun up.

It was a rather sleepy afternoon. Far away I could hear the sound of the advancing beaters – the cries of the boys, the occasional barking of a dog, and the shrill piping of the head- keeper's whistle. Suddenly three birds swung into view round the face of the hill, and made straight for the line of butts. They were just below me, nearer to Standish's butt than mine, but I put up my gun and picked off the nearest. The other two, instead of keeping on their course over Standish's head, suddenly swerved round to the left, almost at right angles – I think they had seen Miss Euncle's tarn o' shanter and simultaneously decided that there are worse things than death – and flew straight down the line, followed by an ineffectual volley from the twelve and twenty - eight bores respectively.

" Now, Dermott, my boy!" I ejaculated, as the birds skimmed past the third butt. " There's a chance for a really pretty right and left."

But no sound – no movement even – came from our crack's lair. The birds flew by unharmed, only to fall later on, one to the Admiral, and one to young Gilmerton.

" *Dormitat Homerus,"* I murmured, gazing curiously towards Dermott's butt. " I wonder if – Jove, there they go! What a pack ! Well done, Gerald! Oh, Gilmerton, you old *sweep!* Fire, man, *fire !* Good old Admiral! Dermott, man, what the devil – – Have *at* them !"

I fairly danced hi the heather. A perfect cloud of birds was pouring over the lower part of the line. The Admiral, the Gilmertons, and Gerald were firing fast and furiously, – even the laird of Nethercraigs loosed off at birds that were neither running nor sitting, – and when the beaters appeared in sight five minutes later, and the drive came to an end, the four lower butts totalled twelve brace among them.

I humbly proffered my solitary contribution.

" Twelve and a half," said the Admiral. " Now, Standish ? "

" N. E. this time," remarked that youth philosophically.

The Admiral said nothing, but I saw his choleric blue eyes slide round in the direction of "Miss Buncle's headgear. He turned to Dermott.

" How many, old man ? "

"Blob!"

That Dermott should return empty-handed from any kind of chase was so surprising that we all turned round for the explanation. Dermott was looking very dejected. This was evidently a blow to his professional pride.

"Didn't any of that great pack come near you ?" asked the Admiral sympathetically.

"No – don't think so," said Dermott shortly.

I had counted eight birds flying straight over his butt myself, but I said nothing. I was beginning to comprehend. *Et ego in Arcadia vixi.*

But the obtuse master-mariner persisted.

"How about that brace that flew right down the line? You must have seen 'em coming all the way. You didn't even try a shot at them, man!"

Dermott, who was fastening up his gaiter, answered rather listlessly –

" Sorry ! It was – a misfire, I think."

"What?" cried the outraged Admiral "A *misfire?* Both barrels – of both guns?"

I did not hear the answer to this. I was looking at Dolly. Her face could not be seen, for she was kneeling down a little distance away, assiduously fondling the silky ears of a highly-gratified red setter. And I realised then that some expressions are capable of a metaphorical as well as a literal interpretation.

IV.

My wife and daughter returned home in the "machine" in time for dinner, without Robin.

" His mother kept him," Kitty explained. She was favouring me with a summary of her day's adventures, in the garden after dinner. " Such an old dear, Adrian I And his father is a grand old man. Very solemn and scriptural-looking and all that, but so courtly and simple when once he gets over his shyness. (He tried to come in to tea in his shirt-sleeves, but his wife hustled him out of the kitchen just in time.) Sir James Fordyce was a shock, though. When we arrived he was chopping turnips in a machine, dressed in clothes like any farm-labourer's. He said it was fine to get back to his own people again. To look athim you would never guess that he was one of the best known men in London, and a favourite at Court, and *such* an old dandy in Bond Street. The rest of the household didn't seem to set any particular store by him. They took him quite as a matter of course."

"What a pity English people can't do the same," I mused. " If they do possess a distinguished relative they brag about him, and he usually responds by avoiding them. If he does honour them with a visit, they try to live up to him, and put on unnecessary frills, and summon all the neighbourhood to come and inspect him."

" There's nothing of that kind about the For- dyces," said Kitty. " Sir James was just one of themselves; he even spoke like them. It was, ' Aye, Jeems !' and ' Aye, John !' all the time."

"How about the rest of the family?" I inquired.

" The mother was immensely pleased to have Robin with her again, I could see," said Kitty. " She made no particular fuss over him, but I'm sure she simply hugged him as soon as we were gone. She had a talk with me about him when we were alone. She seems to regard him as the least successful member of the family, although he has been a good son to them. (Do you know, Adrian, he has sent them something like two hundred pounds during the time he has been with us? And that must have left him little enough to go on with, goodness knows!) But I don't think they consider him a patch on the eldest son, who is a great silent man with a beard – a sort of Scotch John Bidd. He looks years older than Robin, though of course he isn't. He is a splendid farmer, his mother tells me, and greatly " respeckit" in the district. But the poor dear was so frightened of me that he simply bolted from the house the moment he had finished his tea. The sister is pretty, and nice too, but shy. I'm afraid she found my clothes rather overpowering, though I'd only a coat and skirt on. But we got on splendidly after that. She is going to be married next month, to the minister, which is considered an immense triumph for her by the whole community. We must send them a present. By the way, what's the matter with Dolly?"

"What's the matter with poor old Dermott?" I retorted.

At this moment the much-enduring " machine "jingled up to the door, and Captain Dermott's luggage, together with his gun-cases and a generous bundle of game for the mess-table at Aldershot, was piled in at the back. Their owner followed after, and seeing the glowing end of my cigar in the dark, advanced to say good-bye.

Kitty uttered some pretty expression of regret at his departure, and flitted into the house. Dermott and I surveyed each other silently through the darkness.

"Is it any use asking you to come and look us up in town ?" I said at last rather lamely.

He laughed through set teeth – not a pretty sound.

" I think I'll – avoid your household for a bit, Adrian," he answered.

I nodded gravely.

" I see," I said. " I – I'm sorry, old man !"

"I'm going to India, if I can get away," he continued, after a pause.

" Good scheme !" I replied. " We shall think of you most kindly – er, *all* of us."

He said nothing, but shook hands in a grateful sort of fashion, and turned away.

I suppose there is a reason for everything in this world. Still, the spectacle of a good man fighting dumbly with a cruel disappointment – and disappointment is perhaps the bitterest pill in all the pharmacopeia of life – is certainly a severe test of one's convictions on the subject.

At this moment the rest of the party – *minus* Dolly – flowed out on to the doorstep to say farewell; and two minutes later Captain Dermott drove heavily away – back to his day's work.

Well, thank God there is always that!

"I thought she was going to take him," said Kitty in her subsequent summing-up. "It was far and away the best offer she has ever had. And he is such a dear, too! What does the child want, I wonder ! A coronet ?"

" ' A dinner of herbs,' perhaps," said I.

Kitty eyed me thoughtfully, and gave a wise little nod.

"Yes – Dolly is just that sort," she agreed. "But what makes you think that?"

" Oh – nothing," I said.

There are certain matters upon which it is almost an impertinence for a man to offer an opinion to a woman, and I rather shrank from rushing in where my wife had evidently notthought it worth while to tread. Still, I could not help wondering in my heart whether the arrival of one gentleman on Sunday may not sometimes have something to do, however indirectly, with the abrupt departure of another gentleman on Monday.

6

SECTION 6

216
CHAPTER TWELVE.
THE COMPLEAT ANGLER.

The Division of Stoneleigh, which had hitherto done me the honour of returning me as its Member of Parliament, is a triangular tract of country in the north of England.

At the apex of the triangle lies Stoneleigh itself, a township whose chief assets are an ancient cathedral at one end, and a flourishing industry, proclaiming to the heavens its dependence upon Hides and Tallow, at the other. The base of the triangle runs along the sea-coast, and is dotted with fishing villages. Most of the intervening area is under cultivation.

It will be seen, then, that the character of my constituency varied in a perplexing manner, and while I could usually depend upon what I may call the Turnip interest, I could not always count with absolute certainty on the whole-hearted support of the Fish or Hides-and-Tallow.

To this delectable microcosm my household and I migrated one bleak day in February, to commence what promised to be an arduous and thoroughly uncomfortable electoral campaign.

The Government had gone out at last, more from inanition than over any definite question of policy; and we were going to the country to face what is paradoxically termed " the music." It would be a General Election in every sense of the word, for there was no particular question of the hour – this was before the days of Passive Resistance and Tariff Reform – and our chief bar to success would undoubtedly be our old and inveterate enemy, " the pendulum." Of course we were distributing leaflets galore, and blazoning panegyrics on our own legislative achievements over every hoarding in the country – especially where our opponents had already posted up scathing denunciations of the same – and of course we declared that we were going to come again, like King Arthur; but I think most of us realised in our hearts that the great British Public, having decided in its ponderous but not altogether unreasonable way that any change of government must be for the better, was now going to pull us down from the eminence to which we had been precariously clinging forfive years, and set up another row of legislative Aunt Sallies in our stead.

However, we were far from admitting this. We wore our favours, waved our hats, and celebrated our approaching triumph with as great an appearance of optimism as the loss of seven consecutive by-elections would permit.

Our party – Kitty, Phillis, Dolly, and myself: Dilly and Dicky were to follow, and Robin had preceded us by two days – was met at the station by an informal but influential little deputation, consisting of Mr Cash, my agent, a single-minded creature who would cheerfully have done his best to get Mephistopheles returned as member if he had been officially appointed to further that gentleman's interests; old Colonel Vincey, who would as cheerfully have voted for the same candidate provided he wore Conservative colours; Mr Bugsley, a leading linen-draper and ex-Mayor of the town, vice- chairman of our local organisation; Mr Winch – locally known as Beery Bill – the accredited mouthpiece of the Stoneleigh liquor interest; and the Dean, who came, I was uncharitable enough to suspect even as he wrung my hand, on business not unconnected with the unfortunate deficit in the fund for the restorationof the North Transept. There were also present one or two reporters, and a *posse* of the offscourings of Stoneleigh small-boydom.

We drove in state to the hotel. Previous to this I shook hands warmly with the Station- master, who scowled at me – he was a Home- Ruler and a Baptist – and gave four porters half-a-crown apiece for lifting our luggage on to the roof of a cab. I also handed a newsboy sixpence for a copy of the local bi-weekly organ which supported our cause, and tendered half- a-sovereign in payment for a bunch of violets and primroses – our party colours in this district were purple and gold – which were proffered me outside the station by an ancient flower -selling dame who, Cash hissed into my ear, happened to be the mother of four strapping and fully- enfranchised sons; i and presented an unwashed stranger who was holding open the cab door for us with a token of affection and esteem which could readily be commuted into several hours' beer.

On arriving at the hotel I handed the cabman a fare roughly equivalent to the cash value of the cab, and then proceeded to distribute largesse to a crowd of menials who kindly undertook the task of lifting the luggage from the roof andconveying it to our rooms. The horse, having no vote, received no pecuniary return for its labours, but was rewarded for its devotion to Conservative principles by a lump of sugar, which Phillis had been tightly holding in a moist hand ever since Cash had handed it to her at the station – a pretty and thoughtful act of disinterested kindness which was duly noted in the *Stoneleigh Herald* next morning, and effectually secured the votes of several elusive but sentimental wobblers on polling day.

After this unostentatious entry into my constituency I duly established myself in my apartments, where I spent most of the afternoon writing cheques. The restoration of the North Transept proved to be in an even more deplorable state of backwardness than I had feared; but the Dean ultimately left me with the utmost expressions of goodwill, promising to reassure the most exacting spirits in Cathedral society as to my soundness on the questions of (1) Disestablishment and (2) Secular Education in Elementary Schools.

Thereafter I received the captain of the local football team, who begged to remind me that my subscription of five guineas, as Honorary Vice-President of the club, was now due, andfurther requested that I would do himself and colleagues the honour of kicking-off in the match against the Scrappington Hotstuffs on Saturday week. (Saturday next, I heard afterwards, had been reserved for my rival.) He finally departed with my cheque in his pocket, and, I expect, his tongue in his cheek.

Robin next let in upon me a sub-section of the General Purposes Committee of the Municipal Library, who begged that I would kindly consent to open the new wing thereof, jointly with the rival Candidate, at three o'clock next Wednesday ; and intimated as an afterthought that the oak bookcase in the eastern alcove was still unpaid for. They departed calling down blessings upon my head. (Five pounds ten.)

Next, after a brief call from a gentleman in a blue ribbon, who came to solicit a guinea for the Band of Hope, and who left in exchange one hundred copies of a picture of the interior of a drunkard's stomach, executed in three colours, came Beery Bill, to whom the reader has already been introduced. He had not come to talk Politics, he said, but just to have a quiet chat with one whom he hoped he could regard as a personal friend. (I got out my fountain pen.) The chat materialised presently into an intimation that the Licensed Victuallers Benevolent Something-or-Other was short of cash; and my visitor suggested that a trifle in support of the charities of that most deserving institution would come gracefully from my pocket. On handing me the receipt he informed me that the brewing trade was in a bad way, and that he looked to me to do something for it if he used his influence on my behalf at the Election.

The next visitor was an eccentric but harmless old gentleman who eked out a precarious livelihood as a Herbalist – whatever that may be – in the most plebeian quarter of the town. He inhabited a small and stuffy shop up a discreet alley, suffered much from small boys, sold curious drugs and potions of his own composition, and prescribed for persons whose means or modesty precluded them from consulting an orthodox practitioner.

He was threatened, it appeared, with the penalties of the law. He had sold a "love-philtre" (pronounced infallible for recalling errant *fiances* to a sense of duty) to an amorous kitchen-maid who was seeking to rekindle the sacred flame in the bosom of an unresponsive policeman. The damozel had mingled the potion in a plate of beefsteak pudding, and had handedthe same out of the scullery window to her peripatetic swain;

with the sole result that that limb of the law had been immediately and violently sick, and, the moment he felt sufficiently recovered to do so, had declared the already debilitated match at an end. The kitchen-maid, rendered desperate, had told him the whole truth; and consequently my esteemed caller was now wanted by the police.

The catastrophe of the pie, he explained, was in no way to be attributed to the love-philtre (which was composed of sifted sugar and cinnamon), but was due to the fact that instead of the philtre he had inadvertently handed his fair client a packet out of the next drawer, which contained ready-made-up doses of tartaric acid for immediate use in the case of small boys who had swallowed sixpences. *Hinc lacrymce.* In spite of his complete consciousness of his own innocence, he now found himself compelled in a few days' time to defend his conduct in a court of law. The proceedings would cost money, of which he of course possessed little or none. He had called, he said, confident in the hope that I would assist him to defray the expense of vindicating his integrity as a high- class Herbalist by purchasing six bottles of hisworld-renowned specific for neuralgia, from which dread malady he had been informed – quite incorrectly, by the way – that I occasionally suffered. The thirty shillings thus subscribed, together with a few odd coins which he himself had contrived to scrape together during a long life of thrift, would secure the services of a skilled advocate, who would doubtless be able to prove to the satisfaction of justice that no high-class Herbalist would ever dream, save in the way of kindness, of putting tartaric acid into a policeman's beefsteak pudding.

He added, rather inconsequently, that he had voted Conservative at the last three elections, and had moreover persuaded all the other members of the Royal and Ancient Brotherhood of High-class Herbalists to do the same. (One pound ten.)

My last visitor was a seedy individual in corduroys, who asked for a private interview with the Candidate, and, on this favour being granted, informed me in a confidential and husky whisper that he knew of ten good men and true, fully qualified voters, who were prepared to go to the poll on my behalf for the trifling fee of two pound ten a-head and noquestions asked. He was politely but firmly shown into the street. One has to be on the look-out against persons of this type.

I concluded the afternoon by a rather unsatisfactory interview with Mr Cash. He was by nature a boisterous and optimistic person, but on this occasion I found him inclined to be reticent and gloomy. He announced with a shake of the head that my rival was a very strong candidate; and finally, after a certain amount of pressing, admitted that I was not altogether as universally acceptable to my own side as I might have been.

" You are not violent enough, Mr Ingle- thwaite," he said. "You sympathise too much with the point of view of the opposite side. That's fatal."

I turned to Robin.

" You hear that ? " I said. " Don't you ever call me a prejudiced old Tory again, Robin."

"Then," continued the dolorous Cash, "you are too squeamish. Those posters that you wouldn't allow to be put up – that was simply throwing away good votes. Politics in this part of the country can't be played with kid gloves. Then there are the meetings. You don't let the other side have it hot enough. Call 'em robbers and liars I That's what wins an election !"

" I suppose it is," I said mournfully. " Robin, we must put our opinions in our pockets and beat the party drum. Come on, let us go to the Committee Rooms !"

For the next fortnight we worked like galley- slaves. Each morning Kitty and I drove round the town in an open carriage-and-pair decorated with our colours, bowing to such of our constituents as would look at us, and punctiliously returning any salutes we received. Occasionally whole-hearted supporters would give us a cheer, and occasionally – rather more frequently, it seemed to me – disagreeable persons booed at us. Once we were held up outside a hide-and- tallow work by a gang of workmen who wished to address a few questions to the Candidate. "We came well out of that ordeal, for both Kitty and Dolly happened to be in the carriage that day, and they so completely captivated the spokesman of the deputation – no wonder! a pretty woman never looks so attractive as in furs – that that gentleman concluded a catechism of unpremeditated brevity and incoherence by proposing a vote of confidence in, coupledwith three cheers for, Mr Inglethwaite *and* his young ladies!

On another occasion a gnarled and fervent Radical of the bootmaking persuasion hobbled to the door of his establishment, and waving clenched and uplifted fists, called down upon us and our retreating equipage all the curses at the command of a rather extensive vocabulary until we were out of earshot.

Occasionally little girls threw posies into the carriage: little boys, not to be outdone in politeness, threw stones: and altogether I felt very much as the Honourable Samuel Slumkey must have done upon the historic occasion on which he solicited the votes of the electors of the borough of Eatanswill.

Talking of Eatanswill, I had already made the acquaintance of Mr Horatio Fizkin in the person of my opponent, Mr Alderman Stridge, Wholesale Provision Merchant and Italian Warehouseman. His selection as Liberal Candidate was a blow to us: we had hoped for nothing worse than a briefless carpet-bagger from the Temple, as on previous occasions. However, the Alderman on our introduction was extremely affable, and expressed a hope, with the air of one discovering the sentiment for the first time, that the best man might win; to which I, as in duty bound, replied that I hoped not; and we parted with mutual expressions of goodwill and esteem, to deride each other's politics and bespatter each other's characters on countless platforms and doorsteps until we should meet again, after the fray, at the counting of the votes.

On returning from our morning drive (which usually included an open-air meeting) we took luncheon, generally in the presence of various anaemic young men who represented local organs of public opinion, and who expected the long- suffering candidate to set forth his views between mouthfuls of chop and sips of sherry. I usually turned these over to Robin, who understood their ways; and he charmed them, so wisely that even the relentless Cash was compelled to admit that our press notices might have been worse.

Robin was a tower of strength. Indeed he and Dolly were my two chief lieutenants; Dilly and Dicky, as became a pair who had only been married a few months, proving but broken reeds. A week's electioneering proved sufficient for their requirements ; and, declining flatly to " grin like a dog and run about the city" – Dilly's pithysummary of the art of canvassing – any longer, they left us ten days before polling-day to pay a country-house visit. But Robin was everywhere. He answered my letters and he interviewed reporters. He could keep a meeting in hand (pending my arrival from another) with such success that when I finally appeared upon the platform to take up the wondrous tale of my party's perfections, the audience were loth to let Robin go. In six days he acquired a knowledge of the wants, peculiarities, weaknesses, and traditions of my constituents which had occupied all my powers of concentration and absorption for six arduous years. He used to drop into his speeches little topical allusions and local "gags" which, though Greek to the uninitiated, never failed to produce a roar: and a political speaker who can unfailingly make his audience laugh with him – not at him – has gone far on the road to success.

Once, at a meeting, when I was half-way through a speech to an unmistakably bored and rather hostile audience, Robin, who was sitting beside me, slipped a sheet of paper on to my table. The message on the paper, written large for me to read, said – *Compare Stridge to the Old Lady of Dippleton.* What the lady had done I did not know, neither had I time to inquire; but I took my secretary's advice, and, after pausing for a brief drink of water, concluded my sentence –

" – and I maintain, gentlemen, that my opponent, in advocating such a policy as that which he has had the – the – yes, the *effrontery* to lay before a clear-thinking and broad-minded Stoneleigh audience last night, has shown himself to be no wiser in his generation, no better or more statesmanlike in character, than – than – what shall we say ? than " – I glanced at the paper on the table – "the Old Lady of Dippleton!"

There was a great roar of laughter, and I Bat down. I was ultimately awarded a vote of thanks, which should by rights have been given to the heroine of my closing allusion. I may mention here that no subsequent inquiry of mine ever elicited from Robin or any one else what the Old Lady of Dippleton *had* done. Probably it was one of those things that no real lady ever ought to do, and I discreetly left it at that.

Dolly, too, proved a treasure. Her strong line was canvassing. She could ingratiate herself with short-tempered and over-driven wives apparently without effort; surly husbands melted before her smile; sheepish young men forgot the encumbering existence of their hands and feet in her presence; and she was absolutely infallible with babies. Her methods were entirely her own, and gratifyingly free from the superior and patronising airs usually adopted by fine ladies when they go to solicit the votes of that variegated and much-graded community which they cheerfully and indiscriminately sum up as " the lower classes."

Let us follow her as she flits on her way to pay a morning call upon Mr Noah Gulching of Jackson's Row.

Mr Gulching, she finds, is absent in search of a job, while Mrs Gulching, thoroughly cross and worried, is doing the housework with one hand and dangling a fractious teething baby from the other. The rest of the family are engaged in playing games of skill and chance (on the win, tie, or wrangle principle), in the middle of the street outside; and piercing screams 'testify to the fact that John William Gulching, aged two, had just been uprooted by Mary Kate Gulching, who wants to lay out a new Hop-Scotch court, from the flagstone upon which he has been seated for the last half hourand dumped down upon another, the warming of which, even his untutored sensations inform him, will be a matter of some time and trouble.

Dolly, not a whit dismayed by a thoroughly ungracious reception, tucks up her skirt, rolls up her sleeves, finishes washing-up, makes a bed, and peels some potatoes. Then she takes the baby and attends to its more conspicuous wants, what time Mrs Gulching, thoroughly mollified, – she had thought at first that Dolly was "a person with tracks," – goes round the corner to the " Drop Inn," at which hostelry the work of which her spouse is habitually in pursuit invariably goes to ground, and brings that gentleman home with her, to find Dolly playing with a spotless infant whom she gradually recognises as her own offspring.

Dolly begins at once.

"Good morning, Mr Gulching! I expect you think I am one of those horrid canvassers."

Mr Gulching, a little taken aback, admits that such was his impression.

"Well, I'm not," says Dolly. *(Oh, Dotty!)* "I suppose there may be some excuse for canvassing among people who do not take much interest in politics, – though *I* shouldn't like to do it, – but it would be rather a waste of timefor me or any one else to come and try on that sort of thing with *you,* wouldn't it, Mr Gulching?"

Mr Gulching, outwardly frigid but inwardly liquescent, agrees that this is so; and adds in a truculent growl that he would like to see 'em try it on.

"What I really want," continues Dolly, "is your *advice. I* am told that you are so respected here, and have such a knowledge of the requirements of the neighbourhood, that you might be inclined to give us a little help in a scheme which Mr Inglethwaite has in hand. Schemes for the improvement of some of the houses – not snug little cribs like this, but the homes of people who are not so clever and able to take care of themselves as you – and the supplying of more amusements in the evenings; entertainments, lectures "

" Teetotal ? " inquires Mr Gulching hoarsely.

" Oh dear, no. I am sure Mr Inglethwaite would not wish to deprive any one of his glass of beer. He quite agrees with your views' about moderate drinking." (This, I may mention, is a slanderous libel on me, but it sounds all right as Dolly says it.) "But he knows that the success of his efforts will depend entirely uponwhether he has the support of such men as yourself – men who know what they want and will see that they get it. We can't do without you, you see," she adds, with a bewitching little smile.

Visible swelling on the part of Mr Gulching. Dolly gets up.

" Well, I know you are a busy man, Mr Gulching, so I mustn't keep you listening to a woman's chatter any more. I'm afraid I haven't explained things very deeply, but then you men are such creatures for wanting to get to the root of the matter, aren't they, Mrs Gulching ? However, Mr Inglethwaite will call shortly and discuss things with you. I know he wants your advice. Meanwhile, perhaps you will mention the matter to any friends of yours whom you think would be likely to help us, won't you? Good morning, and thank you so much for granting me this – er – interview. An Englishman's house is his castle, isn't it? That is why it was so good of you to let me come in. Good-bye, Mrs Gulching. He's a perfectly sweet little chap, and I must come and see him again, if I may." (The last remark is a little ambiguous, but probably refers to the baby.)

And Dolly, with a friendly nod to the restof the family (who are by this time drawn up *en Echelon* at the street door, under the personal direction of Violet Amelia Gulching), sails out, followed by a gratified leer from the greatly inflated Mr Gulching, having secured that free and independent elector's vote without even having asked for it. And yet some women are crying out for the right to control elections!

At the street corner, with a persuasive finger in the buttonhole of an unconvinced Socialist (and a vigilant eye straining down the long and unlovely vista of Jackson's Row), Dolly usually encounters Robert Chalmers Fordyce.

7

SECTION 7

CHAPTER THIRTEEN.

A HOSTAGE TO FORTUNE.

Nomination day came, and I was duly entered by my proprietors for the Election Stakes, though I was painfully aware that my selection as Candidate was not universally popular.

However, as Cash remarked, " It is canvassing from door to door that does the trick, and there you have the bulge on Stridge. He's not a bad old buffer himself, but they hate his wife like poison. She drives up to their doors in a silver-plated brougham with a double- breasted coachman, and tells 'em to vote for Stridge, not because he used to live in a one- roomed house himself – which he did, and her too – but because he's a local god-on-wheels. Of course they won't stick that."

I also continued to address meetings, receive deputations, and generally solicit patronage in a way that would have made a cab-tout blushfor shame. As a recreation I kicked off at football matches and laid foundation - stones. The most important function in which I took part was the opening of the new wing of the Municipal Library. The ceremony, which was by way of being a non-party affair, took place on a blustering February afternoon. The *Mite* of Stoneleigh were picturesquely grouped upon the steps of the main entrance of the Library, from the topmost of which the

Mayor, the Dean, and the Candidates addressed a shivering and apathetic audience below.

Fortunately, the company were too exclusively occupied in holding on their hats and blowing their blue noses to pay much attention to the improving harangues of Mr Stridge and myself; which was perhaps just as well, for men who have three or four highly critical and possibly hostile meetings to address later in the day are not likely to waste good things upon an assembly who probably cannot hear them, and will only say " Hear, hear 1" in sepulchral tones if they do.

The actual opening of the wing was accomplished quite informally (and I may say unexpectedly) by Kitty and Mrs Stridge – a fearsome matron, who looked like a sort of Nonconform1st Boadicea – who were huddling together for warmth in the recess of the doorway. On a pedestal before them lay two small gold keys, with which they were presently to unlock the door itself, what time I, in trumpet tones, declared the Library open. Whether through natural modesty or a desire to escape the assaults of the wind, the two ladies shrank back so closely into the door that that accommodating portal, evidently deeming it ungallant to wait even for a golden key under such circumstances, incontinently flew open, and Mesdames Ingle- thwaite and Stridge subsided gracefully into the arms of a spectacled and embarrassed Librarian, who was formally waiting inside to receive the company at the proper moment.

After that, the proceedings, which so far had been almost as bleak as the weather, went with a roar to the finish.

But events like these were mere oases in a desert of ceaseless drudgery. The fight grew sterner and stiffer, and, as always happens on these occasions, the neutral and the apathetic began to bestir themselves and take sides. A week before the election there was not an impartial or unbiassed person left in Stoneleigh. Collisions between supporters of either partybecame frequent and serious. On the first occasion, when a Conservative sought to punctuate an argument by discharging a small gin- and-ginger into the face of his Liberal opponent, and the Liberal retaliated by felling the Conservative to the earth with a pint-pot, Stridge and I wrote quite effusively to one another apologising for the exuberance of our friends. A week later, when certain upholders of my cause bombarded Stridge's emporium with an assortment of Stridge's own eggs, hitting one of Mr Stridge's white-jacketed assistants in the eye, and severely damaging the frontage of Mr Stridge's Italian warehouse – whereupon local and immediate supporters of the cause of Stridge squared matters by putting three bombardiers into a horse-trough – Mr Stridge and I expressed no sort of regret to one another whatsoever, but referred scathingly, amid rapturous cheers, at our next meetings to the blackguardly policy of intimidation and hooliganism by which the other side found it necessary to bolster up a barren cause and hopeless future; all of which shows that things were tuning up to concert pitch.

Results of other elections were coming in every day, and they were not by any means favourableto our side. Still, we kept on smiling, and talked largely about the swing of the pendulum – almost as useful a phrase as " Mesopotamia" of blessed memory – and other phenomena of reaction, and hoped for the best. Champion, who had been returned for his constituency by a thumping majority, had promised to come down and speak for me at a great meeting two nights before the election; and Dubberley, who had lost his seat, threatened to come and help me to lose

w' "

mine.

With the exception of Robin, who appeared to be made of some material *(ere perennius,* we were all getting the least bit " tucked up," from my humble self down to Phillis, who appeared at breakfast one morning looking flushed and rather too bright-eyed.

"Electioneering seems to be telling on you, old lady," I remarked. " Feeling quite well – eh?"

"Just a *teeny* headache, daddy. But" – hastily – " I can come with you to the meeting in the theatre to-morrow night, can't I? it will be *such* fun! "

" Meeting ? My little girl, it does not begin till an hour after your bed-time."

" That's why I want to go," said my daughterfrankly. " Besides, I do *love* pantomimes – especially the clowns !" She wriggled ecstatically.

Even the revelation of the plain truth – that the pantomime would be called by another name and the clowns would appear in mufti – failed to assuage Phillis's thirst for the dramatic sensation promised by a meeting in a theatre. I was, as usual, wax in her small hands; and, man-like, I threw the *onus negandi* upon Eve's shoulders.

" Ask your mother," I said; and flew to my day's work.

Thank goodness, it was almost the last. Tomorrow would be the eve of the poll, and at night we were to hold our monster meeting. Three thousand people would be present; a local magnate, Sir Thomas Wurzel (of Heycocks), would occupy the chair; what one of our local reporters insisted on calling "the *elite* of the *bon ton"* would be ranged upon the platform; and the meeting would be addressed by John Champion, Robin, – they always wanted him now, – and the much-enduring Candidate. The audience would, further, be made the recipients of a few remarks from the Chair and (unless something providential happened) from Dubberley, who was to second a vote of thanks to somebody – a performance which might take anything up to fifty minutes. Altogether a feast of oratory, and a further proof, if any were needed, that the English are a hardy race.

Phillis was decidedly unwell next morning, and Kitty prescribed bed. I am inclined to be an anxious parent, but there was little time for the exercise of any natural instincts on this occasion. Hounded on by the relentless Cash, I spent the day in a final house-to-house canvass, being fortunate enough to find at home several gentlemen who had been out on previous occasions, and who now graciously permitted Kitty to present them with a resplendent portrait of what at first eight appeared to be a hairdresser's assistant in gala costume, but which an obtrusive inscription below proclaimed to be "Inglethwaite! The Man You Know, and Who Knows You !"

After a hasty round of the Committee Rooms I returned to our hostelry, the Cathedral Arms, where, after disposing of two reporters who wanted an advance copy of my evening's speech, and having effusively thanked a pompous individual for a sheaf of statistics on a subject which I cannot recall, but in which no one outside an asylum could have reasonably been expected to take any interest whatever, andwhich I was at liberty to quote (with due acknowledgments) to any extent I pleased, I sat down with

Champion and Robin, faint yet pursuing, to fortify myself with roast-beef and whisky for the labours of the evening.

Presently Kitty entered, with Dolly.

" *Who* do you think has just arrived ? " she said.

" I don't know. Not a deputation, I hope!"

" No. Geraldfrom school."

" Great Scott! Expelled ? "

"Oh no. It's his half-term *exeat.* I had forgotten all about it. As it just falls in with the Election, he has come to see you through, he says."

" Bight 1 Give him some food and a bed, and we'll send him round with one of the brakes to-morrow, to bring people up to the poll. He has a gentle compelling way about him that should be useful to us. Has he brought his inarticulate friend ? "

"Yes."

"Well, tell them to ask at the office for bedrooms."

" They have done that already," said Dolly. "They are down in the kitchen now, ordering dinner. They don't propose to go to the meeting. ' Better fun outside,' they say."

"Lucky little devils!" remarked the Candidate, with feeling.

" And, Adrian," said Kitty, " I don't think I'll come either. I'm rather bothered about Philly."

I laid down my knife and fork.

" What do you mean ? Is she really ill ? "

" N - no. I don't think so, but she is very feverish and wretched, poor kiddy. I tried to get hold of Dr Martin this afternoon, but he was miles away on an urgent case, and won't be back till to-morrow. But I got Dr Farquh arson "

"Roaring Radical!" said I in horror-struck tones.

– " Yes, dear, but such a nice old thing; and Scotch too, Robin "

" Aberdonian," said Robin dubiously.

" Well," continued my wife, " he said she would need care, and must stay in bed. He was in a tearing hurry, as he had to go on to one of Stridge's meetings – horrid creature! – but he promised to come again on his way home. Do you think it very important that I should come with you?"

I turned to my secretary.

"What's your opinion, Robin?"

" I think Mrs Inglethwaite should come. They like to see her on the platform, I know."

"If the Candidate's wife does not appear, people say she is too grand for them," put in Champion.

"I'll stay with Philly, Kit," said Dolly.

" Will you ? You dear! But I know you want to come yourself."

"Never mind. It doesn't matter."

And so it was arranged.

We found the theatre packed to suffocation. A heated band of musicians (whose degrees must have been conferred *honoris causa)* had just concluded a set of airs whose sole excuse for existence was their patriotic character, and Sir Thomas Wurzel (of Heycocks) was rising to his feet, when our party appeared on the platform. Election fever was running high by this time; the critical spirit was almost entirely obliterated by a truly human desire to cut the preliminaries and hit somebody in the eye; and we were greeted with deafening cheers.

Presently Champion was introduced and called upon to speak. He was personally unknown to the crowd before him, although his name was familiar to them. But in five minutes he had the entire audience in his grip. He made them laugh, and he made them cheer; he made them breathe hard, and he made them chuckle. Therewere moments when the vast throng sat in death - like silence, while Champion, with his voice dropped almost to a whisper, cajoled them as a woman cajoles a man. Then suddenly he would blare out another battle-call, and provoke a great storm of cheering. He made little use of gesture – occasionally he punctuated a remark with an impressive forefinger, but he had the most wonderful voice I have ever heard. J sat and watched him with whole-hearted admiration. It is true that he was not doing our cause any particular good. He had forgotten that he was there to make a party speech, to decry his opponents, and crack up his friends. He was soaring away into other regions, and – most wonderful of all – he was taking his audience with him. He besought them to be men, to play the game, to think straight, to awaken to a sense of responsibility, and to remember the magnitude and responsibility of their task as controllers of an Empire. He breathed into them for a moment a portion of his own great spirit; and many a small tradesman and dull- souled artisan realised that night, for the first (and possibly the last) time, that the summit of the Universe is not composed of hides and tallow, and that there are higher things than

the loaves and fishes of party politics and the petty triumphs of a contested election.

From a strictly tactical point of view all this was useless, and therefore dangerous. But for a brief twenty minutes we were gods, Utopians, Olympians, joyously planning out a scheme of things as they should be, to the entire oblivion of things as they are. That is always worth something.

Then he sat down, and we came to earth again with a bump, recollecting guiltily the cause for which we were assembled and met together – namely, the overwhelming of an Italian warehouseman and the retention of a parliamentary seat in an unimportant provincial district.

Once only have I heard that speech bettered, and that was in the House of Commons on a night in June fifteen years later, when a Prime Minister started up from the Treasury Bench to defend a colleague whose Bill – since recognised as one of the most statesmanlike measures of our generation – was being submitted to the narrowest and meanest canons of party criticism. It was another appeal for fair-play, unbiassed judgment, and breadth of view, and it took a hostile and captious House, Governmentand Opposition alike, by storm. The name of the Prime Minister on that occasion was John Champion, and the colleague whom he defended was Robert Chalmers Fordyce.

After Champion had sat down – nominally his speech was a vote of confidence in my unworthy self – Robin rose to second the motion. I did not envy him his task. It is an ungrateful business at the best, firing off squibs directly after a shower of meteors. Even a second shower of meteors would be rather a failure under the circumstances. Robin realised this. He put something into his pocket and told his audience a couple of stories – dry, pawky, Scottish yarns – which he admitted were not new, not true, and not particularly relevant. The first was a scurrilous anecdote concerning a man from Paisley, – which illustrious township, by the way, appears to be the target of practically all Scottish humour, – and the other treated of a Highland minister who was delivering to a long-suffering congregation a discourse upon the Minor Prophets. Robin told us how the preacher worked through Obadiah, Ezekiel, Nahum, Malachi, "and many others whose names are doubtless equally familiar to you, gentlemen," he added amid chuckles, placingthem In a kind of ecclesiastical order of merit as he proceeded ; and finally he came to Habakkuk.

" ' What place, my friends, what place will we assign to Habakkuk ?' he roared.

" That, gentlemen," said Kobin, " proved to be the last straw. A man rose up under the gallery.

"' Ye can pit him doon here in my seat,' he roared. ' I'm awa' hame!'

" Gentlemen," added Robin, as the shout of laughter subsided, " I fear that one of you will be for offering *his* seat to Habakkuk if I go on any longer, so I will just second the motion and git down."

After that I rose to my weary feet and offered my contribution. I have no intention of giving a *precis* of my speech here. It was exactly the same as all the speeches ever delivered on such occasions. Thucydides could have written it down word for word without ever having heard me deliver it. It was not in the least a good speech, but it was the sort of speech they expected, and, better still, it was the sort of speech they wanted. Everybody was too excited to be critical, and I sat down, perspiring and thankful, amid enthusiasm.

Then came the moat trying ordeal of all – questions.

I am no hand at repartee; but practice had sharpened my faculties in this direction, and I had, moreover, become fairly conversant with the type of query to which the seeker after knowledge on these occasions usually confines himself. The great secret is to bear in mind the fact that what people want in one's reply is not accurate information – unless, of course, you are standing for a Scottish constituency, and then Heaven help you! – but something smart. If you *can* answer the question, do so; but in any case answer it in such a way as to make the questioner feel small. Then you will have your audience with you.

To prevent unseemly shouting (and, *entre nous,* to give the Candidate a little more time to polish up his impromptus), the questions were handed up on slips of paper and read aloud, and answered *seriatim.* They were sorted and arranged for me by Robin, and I not infrequently found, among the various slips, a question usually coming directly after a regular poser, in Robin's handwriting, with a brilliant and telling reply thoughtfully appended.

This evening as usual Robin collected the slips from the stewards, and ultimately laid them on the table before me. I rose, and started on theheap. The first was a typewritten document which had been handed up by a thoughtful- looking gentleman in the front row. It contained a single line –

Are you a Liberal or a Conservative f

This was a trifle hard, I thought, coming directly after my speech; but fortunately the audience considered it merely funny, and roared when I remarked pathetically, " This gentleman is evidently deaf."

Then came the question –

Are you in favour of Woman's Suffrage ?

This was no novelty, and was fortunately regarded by the gallant electors present as a form of comic relief. I adopted my usual plan under the circumstances, and said –

" I am in favour, sir, of giving a woman whatever she wants. It is always well to make a virtue of necessity."

This homely and non-committal gibe satisfied most of the audience, and I was about to proceed to the next question when my interlocutor, a litigious-looking man with blue spectacles, rose in the circle and cried –

"You are evading the question, sir! Give me an answer. Are you in favour of Woman's Suffrage or not ?"

"That's fair! Give him his answer!" came the cry from the fickle audience.

I was quite prepared for this. I went through an oft-rehearsed and not uneffective piece of pantomime with Kitty, and replied –

" Well, sir, I have just inquired of my wife, who is by my side "

I paused expectantly. I was not disappointed. There were loud cheers, during which I seized the opportunity to glance through the next few questions. Then, as I was not quite ready –

" – As she has *always* been, all through this arduous campaign "

Terrific enthusiasm, while Kitty blushes and bows very prettily; after which the conversation proceeds on the following lines: –

Myself. And she tells me that she does not want any Suffrage of any kind whatso-ever!

" *Hear, hear I" But some cries of disapproval.*

Myself. I therefore recommend you, sir, to go home and follow my example

(Perfect tornado of laughter. Apparently I have made a home-thrust.)

– And after that, if you will come back to me and report the result of your – er – investigations – *(yells)* – I shall be happy to go into the matter with yeu more fully.

Triumphant cheers, and the blue-spectacled man collapses.

The unfortunate espouser of the cause of the fair having thus been derided out of court, I took up the next question. It concerned a longstanding dispute as to the rights of the clergy of various denominations to enter the local Board Schools, – this was in the days far preceding the present educational deadlock, – and I felt that I must walk warily. I talked at large about liberty of conscience and religious toleration, but realised as I rambled on that my moderate views and want of bigotry in one direction or the other were pleasing no one. John Bull is a curious creature. You may get drunk and beat your wife, and he will tolerate you; you may run amok through most of the Decalogue, and he will still be your friend; but venture to worship your Maker in a fashion which differs one tittle from his own, and he will put down his pint-pot or desist from sanding the sugar and fell you to the earth. I was glad to get awayfrom this subject, leaving the audience far from satisfied, and turn to the next question. It said –

Is the Candidate aware that the important township of Spratling is entirely without a pier or jetty of any description f

" Certainly I am aware of it," I replied, trying hard to remember where the place was. The audience began to titter, and I felt uneasy.

My questioner, a saturnine gentleman in the pit, rose to his feet and continued –

" And if returned to Parliament, will you exert your influence to see that a jetty is constructed there at the earliest opportunity ?"

" Cer " There was a very slight movement beside me. Robin was leaning back unconcernedly in his chair, but on the table under my nose lay a sheet of paper bearing these words in large printed capitals –

SPEATLING IS TEN MILES FEOM
THE SEA1

It had been a near thing.

"Certainly," I continued. "On one condition only," I added at the top of my voice, above the rising tide of mocking laughter, – " on condition that you, sir, will personally guarantee a continuous and efficient service of fast steamers between Spratling and – the sea- coast !"

It was not a brilliant effort. I think I

could have made more of it if I had had more time. But it served. How they laughed!

But there were breakers ahead. The next question asked if I was in favour of compulsory land purchase and small holdings. Of course I was not; but if I said so I knew I should rouse a dangerous storm, for the community were much bitten at the time with the "Vine and Fig-tree Fetish," as some one had happily described it. If, on the other hand, I said Yes, I should, besides telling a lie, – though, as Cash once remarked to me, "You can't strain at gnats on polling - day," – be committing myself to a scheme, which I knew Stridge had been strongly urging, for dividing up some of the estate of the Lord of the Manor, the Earl of Carbolton (whom I knew personally for one of the wisest and most considerate landlords in the country) into allotments for the benefit of an industrial population who probably thought that turnips grew on trees. It would have been easy to make some easily broken promise, but I have my poor pride, and I never offer the most academic blessing to a measure that I am not prepared to go into a Lobby for. I wanted time to thinl$. Perhaps Robin would slip something on tothe table. I accordingly played my usual card, and said –

"Now this, gentleman, is an important question, and I am very glad it has been asked." (Oh, Adrian, my *boy!*) "And when I *am* faced with such a question, I always ask myself, 'What, under the circumstances, would be the course of action of – our great leader?'"

The device succeeded, and the theatre resounded with frenzied cheers. I turned to Robin. He was not there.

I swung round in Kitty's direction. She had left her chair, and was hurriedly making her way through the group of important nobodies behind me in the direction of the wings. Robin was there already, in earnest conversation with a girl.

It was Dolly,
Phillis?

8

SECTION 8

257

CHAPTER FOURTEEN.
MTO DIE WILL BE AN *AWFULLY* BIO
ADVENTUBE!"
– *Peter Pan.*

Two minutes later we were driving back to the Cathedral Arms. It was snowing heavily, but I never noticed the fact. Neither did I realise that I had abandoned my post at a critical and dangerous moment, and left my friends on the platform to explain to a puzzled and angry audience why the Candidate had run away without answering their questions. But there are deeper things than politics.

Phillis, we learned from Dolly, had been attacked by violent pains early in the evening; and about nine o'clock there had been a sudden rise of temperature, with slight delirium, followed by a complete and alarming collapse. Dr Farquharsou had been sent for, hot-foot,

from Stridge's platform, and his first proceeding had been to summon me from mine.

He was waiting for us in the hall of the hotel when we arrived, and Kitty and I took him into our sitting-room and, parent-like, begged to be told "the worst."

The doctor – a dour and deliberate Scot – declined to be positive, but " doubted" it might be perityphlitis. "Appendicitis is a more fashionable term," he added. The child had rallied, but was very ill, and nothing more could be done at present except keep her warm and afford relief by means of poultices and fomentations until the malady should take a definite turn for the better or the worse.

"In either case we shall know what to do then," he said; " but for the present the bairn must just fight her own battle. Has she good health, as a rule "

Yes, thank God! she had. Physically she was frail enough, but she possessed a tough little constitution. After I had taken a peep into the room where the poor child, a vision of tumbled hair and wide bright eyes, lay moaning and tossing, I left Kitty and Dolly and the doctor to do what they could for her, and went downstairs to take counsel with my friends.

Now that the first shock was past, my head was clear again, and my course lay plain before me. Downstairs I found Eobin, Champion, and Cash silently taking supper.

" Now, gentlemen," I said, when I had answered Robin's anxious inquiries – I believe he loved the child almost as much as I did – "this misfortune has come at a bad time; but one thing is quite plain, and that is that I must go through with the election. I quite see that I am not my own master at present."

Cash looked immensely relieved. Evidently he had been afraid that I would throw up the sponge. Robin and Champion nodded a grave assent, and the latter said –

"You are right, Adrian. It's the only thing to do."

"That's true," said Cash. "I am sure you have our deepest sympathy, Mr Inglethwaite, but we can't possibly let you off on any account."

It was not a very happy way of putting it, but Cash was an election agent first and a man afterwards.

" It was bad enough your running away from the meeting to-night," he continued, in tones which he tried vainly to keep from sounding reproachful. " They'd have torn the benches up if Mr Fordyce hadn't let 'em have it straight. I'm afraid it will cost us votes to-morrow."

All this grated a good deal. I could hear Robin begin to breathe through his nose, and I knew that sign. I broke in –

"What did you say to them, Robin?"

" Say ? I don't really know. I assured them that you must have some good reason for leaving in such a hurry, and persuaded them to keep quiet for a bit in case you came back. We put up a few more speakers, but the people got more and more out of hand; and finally, after about five minutes of Dubberley, they grew so riotous that we ended the meeting."

"They had every excuse," said L "They considered themselves defrauded."

"So they were," said Cash.

" Of course, if they had *known,"* said Champion, "they would have gone home like lambs."

" Somehow," said Robin, " I wish they could have been told, Adrian. I should have liked fine to explain to them that you didn't leave the meeting just because you couldn't answer that last question."

"By gum!" Cash had been striving to deliver himself for some time. " Mr Inglethwaite," he said excitedly, " they must be told at once! We can get more good out of your little girl's illness than fifty meetings would do us. You know what tho British public are ! I'll circulate the real reason of your departure from the meeting first thing to-morrow morning, and half the wobblers in the place will vote for you out of sheer kind-heartedness. I know 'em ! "

The exemplary creature almost smacked his lips.

There was a tense silence all round the table. Then I said, with some heat –

" Mr Cash, I have delivered myself into your hands, body and soul, ever since Nomination Day, and I have obeyed you to the letter all through this campaign. But – I am not going to allow a sick child's sufferings to be employed as a political asset to-morrow."

There was a sympathetic growl from the other two.

" Oh, we shouldn't do it as publicly as all that," said the unabashed Cash. "Trust mel No ostentation; just an explanatory report circulated in a subdued sort of way – and perhaps a strip of tan - bark down on the road outside the hotel – eh ? *I* know how to do it. It'll pay, I tell you. And there'll be no publicity "

I laid my head upon the table and groaned. For three weeks I had had perhaps four hours' sleep a-night, and I had been worked down to my last reserve of energy, keeping in hand just enough to meet all the probable contingencies of to-morrow's election. Dialectics with Cash as to the market value of a little girl's illness had not been included in the estimate. I groaned.

Champion answered for me.

"Mr Cash, don't you see how painful these proposals are to Mr Inglethwaite ? Put such ideas out of your head once and for all. No man worthy of the name would accept votes won in such a way."

There was a confirmatory rumble from Robin.

"We can't have *ad misericordiam* appeals here, Mr Cash," he said.

Champion continued briskly –

" Now, Mr Cash, we will get Mr Inglethwaite a drink and send him to bed. He has not had a decent night's rest for a fortnight. We trust to you not to talk of the child's illness to anybody, – that is the *only* way to avoid making capital of it, – and if you will call here to-morrowafter breakfast I will guarantee that your Candidate will be fit and ready to go round the polling- booths with you, and" – he put his hand on my shoulder – " set an example to all of us."

Cash, completely pulverised, departed as bidden, desolated over this renunciation of eleemosynary votes ; and Robin, Champion, and I finished our supper in peace, – if one can call it peace when there is no peace.

Champion was leaving by the night mail, for he had promised to address a meeting two hundred miles away next day. His cab was already at the door, and we said good-bye to him on the hotel steps.

He shook hands with me in silence, and turned to Robin.

"Three fingers, and not too much soda, and then put him straight to bed," he commanded.

Then he turned to me again.

"Don't sit up and worry, old man," he said. "Go to bed, anyhow. The doctor and your womenfolk will do all that can be done. *Your* duties commence to-morrow. Keep your tail up, and face it out. *Noblesse oblige,* you know. Good-night."

He drove away, and Robin and I returned to the sitting-room.

Robin mixed me a stiff whisky-and-soda.

"Champion's prescription," he said. "Down with it !"

I obeyed listlessly.

" Now come along upstairs with me. You are going to bed. I want to turn you out a first-class Candidate in the morning – not a boiled owl."

His cheery masterfulness had its effect, and I suddenly felt a man again.

" Never fear !" I said. " I shall go through with it right enough – the whole business – unless – unless – Robin, old man, supposing – supposing "

"Blethers!" said Robin hastily. "She'll be much better in the morning. Here's your room. Good-night!"

He shepherded me into my bedroom, shut the door on me, and tiptoed away.

I really made a determined effort to go to bed. I actually lay down and covered myself up, but sleep I could not. After an hour of conscientious endeavour I rose, inspired with a new idea.

The doctor had straitly forbidden me to enter Phillis's room; but opening out of it was the apartment that was used as her nursery. Therewould be a fire there : I would spend the rest of the night on a sofa in front of it.

I looked at my watch. It was one o'clock. I took a candle, walked softly down the passage, and let myself quietly into the nursery. The door leading into Phillis's room was ajar, and a slight smell of some drug or disinfectant assailed my sharpened senses.

The room was in darkness, except that a good fire burned in the grate. A silent figure rose up from before it at my entrance.

It was Robin. Somehow I was not in the least surprised to see him there.

"Come along," he said softly. "I was expecting you."

We sat there for the rest of the long night. The house was very still, but every quarter of an hour the Cathedral chimes across the Close – our rooms lay in a quiet wing of the hotel, which formed a hollow square with the Cathedral, Chapter-house, and Canonries – furnished a musical break in the silence. So tensely mechanical does one's brain become under such circumstances, that presently I found myself anticipating the exact moment when the next quarter would strike; and I remember feeling quite disappointed and irritable if, when I said to myself " *Now!*" the chime did not ring out for another fifteen seconds or so. Truly, at three o'clock on a sleepless morning the grasshopper is a burden.

Once Robin rose softly to his feet and turned towards the door of Phillis's room. I had not heard any one move there, but when I looked round Dolly was standing on the threshold. She was wrapped in a kimono, – I remember its exact colour and pattern to this day, and the curious manner in which the heraldic - looking animals embroidered upon it winked at me in the firelight, – and she held an incongruous - looking coal-scuttle in her hand. It was not by any means empty, but she handed it to Robin with a little nod of authority and vanished again.

I looked listlessly at Robin, wondering what he was to do with the coal-scuttle. He began to cut a newspaper into strips, after which he picked suitable lumps of coal out of the scuttle and tied them up into neat little paper packets, half a dozen of which he presently handed through the door to Dolly. I suppose she placed them noiselessly on the fire in Phillis's room, but we heard no sound.

It was a bitterly cold night, and outside the snow was lying thick; so Robin busied himself with preparing other little packets of coal, and at intervals throughout the long night he passed them through the door to the tireless Dolly.

Various sounds came from within. Occasionally the child suffered spasms of pain, and we could hear her crying. Then all-wise Nature would grant the sorely tried little body a rest at the expense of the mind that ruled it, and poor Phillis would drop into a sort of rambling delirium, through which we perforce accompanied her. At one time she would be wandering through some Elysian field of her own; we heard her calling her mates and proposing all manner of attractive games. (Even " Beckoning " was included. Once I distinctly heard her "choose" me.) But more often she was in deadly fear. Her solitary little spirit was too plainly beset by those nameless ghosts that haunt the borderland separating the realms of Death from those of his brother Sleep. Once her voice rose to a scream.

"Uncle Robin! It's the Kelpie! Stop it! It's coming – it's breaving on me! Uncle *Robin!* oh 1"

I looked at Robin. He was sitting gripping the arms of his chair, with every muscle in his body rigid; and I knew that he, like myself, was praying God to strike down the cowardly devil that would torment a child.

Then I heard, for the first time that night, the soothing murmur of Kitty's voice.

"It's all right, dearie. Mother is holding you fast. It shan't hurt you. There, it's running away now, isn't it ? See!"

Kitty's tones would have lightened the torments [of the Pit, and Phillis's cries presently died down to an uneasy whisper. After a sudden and curiously pathetic little outburst of singing, – chiefly a jumble of scraps from such old favourites as "Onward, Christian *Sailors!"* – there was silence again, and the Cathedral chimed out half-past four.

Shortly after this the doctor came out of the room with a message from Kitty that I ought to be in bed. Evidently Dolly had told her about me.

"How is she now, doctor?" I whispered, disregarding the command.

" Up and down, up and down. She is making a brave fight of it, poor lassie, but we can do little at present except stand by and give relief when the bad fits come."

" May I go in and see her ?"

"No, no! You could do no good, and she might be frightened if she caught sight of a large dim figure in the dark. Leave it to the women, and thank God for them. Hark !"

Phillis was back in Elysium again.

"Who's been eating my porridge?" said a gruff little voice. Then came a rapturous shriek. Evidently the Little Bear had caught Curly Locks in his bed. We sat listening, while the game ended and another followed in its place. Suddenly she began to sing again –

"Then three times round went that gallant ship,

And three times round went she ;

Then three times round went that gallant ship,

And – sank – to the – bottom of the sea – ea – ee –

There was a little wailing *rallentando,* and silence.

"Philly, Philly, *don't!"* It was the only time that night that Kitty gave any sign of breaking down. The doctor hurried back into the room. The clock struck five.

After that there was a very long silence. It must have lasted nearly an hour. Then Dolly tiptoed out to us.

" She's asleep," she whispered. " He says she's a shade better. I want another coal-packet."

She took what Robin gave her, and faded away.

After that I think we dozed in Out chairs. The next thing I remember was a knock at the outer door. I opened my heavy eyes and stirred my stiff joints. The Boots put his head in, and I realised it was daylight.

" Half-past eight, sir. Mr Cash is waiting downstairs. Poll's been open half an hour, he says." 271

CHAPTER FIFTEEN.

TWO BATTLES.

Before I left the hotel I struck a bargain with Cash. I would go anywhere and do anything, but he was to give me a written itinerary of my movements for the day, clearly stating where I should be at various times. This document I left in the hands of Dolly, who promised faithfully to send for me, if – if necessary.

Then, putting my paternal instincts into my pocket, I braced myself up and plunged into the vortex of polling-day.

Truly, if Time is the healer, Work is the anaesthetic. In the turmoil of the crowded streets and polling - booths, I found myself almost as enthusiastic and whole-hearted as if no little girl of mine were fighting for life in a darkened room not many streets away. I shook hands with countless folk, I addressed meetings of the unwashed at street corners, and received the plaudits or execrations of the multitude with equal serenity.

Robin hastened away to the Hide-and-Tallow Works, whence, during the dinner-hour, he charmed many an oleaginous elector to come and plump for Inglethwaite, the Man Whom He Knew and Who Knew Him. Gerald and Donkin, smothered in violets and primroses, were personally conducting a sort of tumbril, which dashed across my field of vision from time to time, sometimes full, sometimes empty, but always at full gallop.

Election " incidents" were plentiful. I was standing in the principal polling - station at one time, when a gentleman called Hoppett, a cobbler by persuasion – I think I have already mentioned him as the benignant individual who used to come to the door of his establishment and pursue me with curses down the street – came out from recording his vote. He did not see me, but caught sight of Robin, who had just arrived with a *posse* of electors, and was standing by the Returning Officer's table. Hobbling up, the cobbler shook a gnarled fist under my secretary's nose.

" I've voted against your man," he shouted. "We're goin' to be rid of the lot of you thistime. Set of reskils! . . . I've put my mark against Stridge, I have; and against Ingle- thwaite's name I've put a picture of a big boot – one of my own making, too! The big boot!" he screamed ecstatically – " that's what your man is a-going to get to-day. Set of "

Robin smiled benignantly upon him, and glanced at the Returning Officer.

"You hear what this gentleman says?" he remarked.

" I do," replied the official.

" Is it not a fact that he has annulled his vote by making unnecessary marks on his voting- paper ?" continued Robin solemnly.

"That is so," assented the Returning Officer. "I'm afraid your vote won't count this time, Mr Hoppett. Good morning!"

There was a roar of delighted laughter from friend and foe, and the fermenting Hoppett was cast forth.

I succeeded in getting back to the hotel for ten minutes at luncheon-time. Dolly met me – pale, sleepless, but unbeaten.

"The doctor is with her just now," she said. " She has been in fearful pain, poor kiddy; but he has given her a drug of some sort, and she

is easier now."

" Couldn't I see her, just a moment ?" I said wistfully.

"The answer to that question, sir," replied Dolly, "is in the negative."

We both smiled resolutely at this familiar tag, and Dolly concluded –

"Kitty is lying down. I made her. But she is going to get up when they – I mean "

I detected a curious confusion in her voice.

" When what ? " I asked.

"Nothing."

I surveyed my sister-in-law uneasily,

" Are they expecting – a crisis, then ?"

" Yes – a sort of one."

"When?"

Dolly seemed to consider.

" About five," she said.

" Hadn't I better be near, in case ? "

" Where are you to be this afternoon ? "

" Hunnable."

Dolly nodded her head reflectively.

" When can you be back ? " she asked. '" I can do it by five, I should think."

" That will be soon enough. The doctor said that if – you were wanted, it would be about then. Good-bye, old gentleman!"

"Good-bye, Dolly! Mind you go to bed."(We seem to have spent a large portion of that twenty-four hours urging each other to go to bed.)

Then I went back to work.

Polling had been brisk during the dinner- hour, and both Cash and Robin considered that we were doing fairly well. Things would be slack at Stoneleigh itself during the afternoon, and the obvious and politic course now was to drive over to the fishing village of Hunnable – I had only time for one, and this was the most considerable – and catch my marine constituents as they emerged from the ocean, Proteus-like, between three and four o'clock.

I did so, and for the space of an hour and a half I solicited the patronage of innumerable tarry mariners, until their horny hands had filled up the voting-papers and my own smelt to heaven of fish. It was a quarter to five, and dark, before I escaped from the attentions of a small but pertinacious group of inquirers who wanted to understand my exact attitude on the question of trawling within the three- mile limit, and proceeded at a hand - gallop back to Stoneleigh. (That odoriferous but popular vehicle, the motor-car, was still in the preceded - by - a - man - ten - yards - in - front - bearing -a-red-flag stage in those days, and we had to rely on that antiquated but much more Tenable medium of transport, the horse.) The snow lay very heavily in places, and our progress was not over - rapid. Moreover, passing the central Committee Rooms on my way to the hotel, I was stopped and haled within to conciliate various wobblers, and another twenty minutes of precious time sped. But I stuck to my determination to let nothing interfere with duty that day, and I argued with free-thinkers and pump-handled bemused supporters until all was settled and Cash said I might go.

Still, it was nearer six than five when my panting horses drew up at the Cathedral Arms.

There was no Dolly to receive me this time, but at the top of the stairs leading to Out rooms I met the doctor. He was accompanied by a grey-haired, kind-eyed old gentleman in a frock-coat, with " London Specialist" written all over him. It was Sir James Fordyce.

" Well ? " I asked feverishly as I shook hands.

The two men motioned me into the sitting- room, and Farquharson said, in a curiously uncertain fashion –

"Mr Inglethwaite, we have done a thing which should not, properly, have been donewithout your consent. Your secretary suggested the idea, and I agreed. Mrs Inglethwaite made a point of our saying nothing to you, and volunteered to take all responsibility on herself. She said you were not to be worried. So I wired for Sir James "

" I see," I said, " and he operated ? "

" Yes, at three o'clock this afternoon. Indeed, your sister-in-law, I think, purposely concealed from you "

" She did." That, then, was the " crisis " that Dolly had in her mind, and that, too, was why she had told me to come back at five – when everything would be well over!

I continued –

"And how have you – I mean – is she ?"

" The operation," said the old man, " was entirely successful, and, as it turned out, most necessary. But of course for so young a patient the strain was terrible."

" How is she ?"

" She came through finely, but I do not conceal from you the fact that her life hangs by a thread."

I had a premonition that something was going to be " broken " to me. I dropped into a chair, and waited dully. Then I felt a hand on my shoulder, and Sir James continued –

" Just weakness, you understand!   Her exhaustion when she came out of the chloroform was extreme, but every moment now is in our favour. Children have such extraordinary recuperative power."

He was speaking in the usual cheery tones of the bedside optimist. I raised my head.

"Tell me straight, Sir James – will the child live?"

The old man's grip on my shoulder tightened just for a moment, and when he spoke it was in an entirely unprofessional voice.

" Thanks to two of the bravest and most devoted of women," he said, " I think she will."

I dropped my head into my hands.

" Please God !" I murmured brokenly.

" Of course," he continued, " anything may happen yet. But the way in which she has been cared for by my good friend here "

"No, no," said Farquharson. "Give the credit to those that deserve it. I just afforded ordinary professional assistance. It was your wife and her sister, Mr Inglethwaite, that pulled the child through. She has had tight hold of a hand of one of them ever since ten o'clock last night."

"Yes," said Sir James; "I think it will befound that their nursing has just made the difference. You had better give him something, Farquharson."

In truth I needed something, though up to this point I had not realised the fact. Farquharson gave me a draught out of a little glass, which sent a steadying glow all through me, and presently I was able to shake hands, dumbly and mechanically, with the great surgeon, who, I found, was bidding me good-bye; for the world is full of sick folk, and their champion may nob stay to see the issue of one battle before he must hurry off to fight another.

They left me to myself, while Farquharson went down to the door with Sir James. Presently he returned.

"I must be getting back to the patient shortly," he said. " The next hour or so will be very critical. The nurse is here, and I have sent the ladies to bed. But you may go in for a look, if you like. I am going out for exactly ten minutes."

" I see – a breather. You deserve it."

" Not exactly. I'm going to vote – for Stridge!"

He chuckled in a marvellously cheering way, and left me.

As I approached Phillis's room the dooropened, and I was confronted with that most soothing and comforting of sights to a sick man – a nurse's uniform. She was a pleasant-faced girl, I remember, and she was carrying a basin full of sponges and water, cruelly tinged.

" Just a peep!" she said, with that little air of motherly sternness which all women, however young, adopt towards fractious children and helpless males.

She closed the door very softly upon me, and left me alone.

For a moment I stood uncertain in the shadow of the screen that guarded the door. There was a whiff of chloroform in the air, and through the doorway leading to the room where we had sat throughout the previous night I could see the end of a white-covered table. Thank God, that part of the business was over!

A shaded lamp burned at Phillis's bedside. She lay deathly still, an attenuated little derelict amid an ocean of white bed-clothes.

At first I thought I was alone with the child, and was moving softly forward when I became suddenly aware that some one was kneeling at the far side of the bed. It was Kitty. Evidently she had not obeyed the doctor's orders about going to bed.

A single ray from the lamp fell upon her face. Her eyes were wide open, and she seemed to be looking straight at me. Her lips were moving, and I became aware that she was speaking, very earnestly and almost inaudibly.

I stood still to hear her. Then I realised that her words were not addressed to me. Very carefully I stepped back to the door-handle, turned it, and slipped out.

9

SECTION 9

282

CHAPTER SIXTEEN.
"JUI PEKD, OAGNB."

Once more I was back in the thick of it all, and till the closing of the poll at eight o'clock I strove, in company with Cash, Robin, and others, to direct the inclinations of my constituents into the proper channels.

The tumult increased as the evening advanced. More snow had fallen during the afternoon, and outlying electors were being conveyed to the scene of action with the utmost difficulty. People were voting at seven o'clock who had intended to get it done and be home by six; and as time wore on it was seen that there would be a desperate rush of business right up till closing time.

Every one was in high spirits. That potent factor in British politics, the electioneering egg, had been entirely superseded by the snowball, and the youth of Stoneleigh, massed in thepublic square outside the Town Hall, were engaged, with a lofty indifference to party distinctions that would have been sublime if it had not been so painful, in an untrammelled bombardment of all who crossed their path.

At length the Cathedral chimed out the hour of eight, and the poll closed. Cash hurried up to me.

"It's going to be a desperately close thing," he said. "The counting will begin at once, in the Mayor's room on the first floor of the Town Hall. The outlying boxes should be in by half- past nine at the latest, and the result should be out by about eleven. You'll come and watch the counting, I suppose."

But there are limits to human endurance.

"Mr Cash," I said, buttoning my overcoat up to my ears as a preliminary to an encounter with the budding statesmen outside, "I think I have got to the end of my day's work. Nothing can affect the result now, and I'm going home – that's flat. Good-night!"

"Surely you're coming to hear the result announced," wailed Cash. " There's the vote of thanks to the Returning Officer. You'll have to propose that – or second it," he added grimly.

"Well, I'll see. But I think, now that thepoll Is closed, that my duty lies elsewhere," I said. "If I am really wanted, send word by Mr Fordyce."

Five minutes later, and I was once more at the Cathedral Arms. The ground floor of that hostelry hummed like a hive, and the bar and smoking-room were filled to overflowing with supporters of both sides, who were prudently avoiding all risk of disappointment by celebrating the result of the election in advance.

I pushed my way through a group of enthusiastic patriots – many of them in that condition once described to me by a sporting curate as "holding two or three firkins apiece" – who crowded round me, fired with a desire to drink success to the British Constitution – a rash shibboleth, by the way, for gentlemen in their situation to attempt to enunciate at all – at my expense, and hastened upstairs to our wing.

In the passage I met the nurse. She greeted me with a little smile; but I was mistrustful of professional cheerfulness that night.

"Will you tell Mrs Inglethwaite or Miss Rubislaw that I have come in, please?" I said, and turned into the sitting-room.

The sight of a snug room or a bright fire ora colossal arm-chair is always comforting to a weary man, even though his thoughts admit of little rest. I sank down amid these comforts, and closed my eyes. Now that my long day's play-acting was over, and nothing mattered any more, I began to realise how great the strain had been. I was utterly done. I had no clear recollection of having tasted food since breakfast, but I was not hungry. All I wanted was to be left in peace. Even the sickening anxiety about Phillis had died down to a sort of dull ache. In a few minutes a too-wakeful mind struggled with an exhausted body. I wondered dimly when somebody would come and tell me how PhiHy was. Perhaps

I fell asleep.

I was awakened by the consciousness of a second presence in my arm-chair, which was a roomy one of the saddle-bag variety. It was Kitty. Presently I became aware that she was crying, softly, as women usually do, – men gulp noisily, because they have lost control of themselves, and children wail, chiefly to attract attention, – but Bo softly on this occasion that I knew she was trying to avoid disturbing me.

It had happened, then.

Well, obviously, this was one of the rareoccasions upon which a husband can be of some use to his wife. I sat up, and made a clumsy effort at a caress.

"We've still got each other," I said, rather brokenly.

Kitty positively laughed.

" Adrian, you don't understand. Philly roused up for a few minutes about eight o'clock, – very *piano,* poor mite, but almost herself, – and then dropped off into a beautiful sleep, bless her! The doctor has gone home and left the nurse in charge. He says things should be all right now. Oh, Adrian, Adrian !"

And my wife sobbed afresh.

" Then what the – what on earth are you crying for ? " I demanded.

"I don't know, dear," said Kitty, without making any attempt to stop. " I'm so happy!"

Really, women are the most extraordinary creatures. Here was I, after the labour and anxiety of the last twenty-four hours, ready to shout for joy. I was no longer tired: I felt as if my day's work had never been. I wanted to sing – to dance – to give three cheers in a whisper. And my wife, after giving me a very bad fright, was sitting celebrating our victory by a flood of tears and other phenomenausually attributed by the masculine mind to unfathomable woe. It was all very perplexing, and I felt a trifle ill-used; but I suppose it was one of the things that mark the difference between a man and a woman.

After that we sat long and comfortably. Our conversation need not be set down here, for it has no bearing on this chronicle.

Finally we looked at the clock, and then at each other.

" We must have been sitting here a long time," I said. " I wonder where the others are."

" By the way," said Kitty, " Dilly and Dicky have arrived. Robin and Dolly wired for them this morning. They may be upstairs any moment. They were having supper in the coffee- room when last I saw them." She patted her hair. "Do I look an awful fright?"

I turned in the restricted space at my command and surveyed her.

" Do my eyes look wet ? " she inquired, feeling in my pocket for my handkerchief.

Kitty has large grey eyes. Once, during the most desperate period of our courtship, I referred to them as "twin lakes" – an indiscretion which their owner, in her less generous moments, still casts up to me. But to-night the territorysurrounding them presented a distinct appearance of inundation. I continued to gaze. I thought of last night's ceaseless vigil and today's long-drawn battle. My wife had borne the brunt of all, and I had grudged her a few tears! My heart smote me.

"Kit!" I said suddenly; "poor Kit!" . . .

We were interrupted by the opening of the door and the entrance of what I at first took to be a chimney-sweep's apprentice, but which proved to be my brother-in-law, with evidence of electoral strenuousness written thick upon him.

" Hallo, you two!" he remarked genially. Then, noticing our unconventional economy of sitting - space – " Sorry ! I didn't know. I thought you'd given up that sort of thing years ago !" . *"* ;!:-

I rose and *f*. myself.

"Come in, myon," I said.

" Righto !" replied Gerald. Then he addressed himself to a figure which, with true delicacy of feeling, had shrunk back into the passage outside.

" Come in, Moke, old man. I've got them separated now!"

The discreet Master Donkin sidled respectfully in at the door, and Gerald continued.

" Moke and I would like to say how pleasedwe are to hear about Phillis," he said, rather awkwardly for him. "We have just got to hear how really bad she's been."

The resolution was seconded by a confirmatory mumble from Master Donkin.

"We met the nurse just now," continued Gerald, " and she told us about the operation, and all that. It must have been a pretty thick day for you, Adrian. And you're looking pretty rotten, too, Kitty," he added with brotherly directness. " But do you people know what time it is? Half-past eleven, nearly. The result should be out any minute. Aren't you coming to the Town Hall ? They'll want you to make a speech, or get egged, or something."

I looked at my watch.

"Well, there's no partir reason why I shouldn't go – *now"* I said Tfhat do you say, Kitty? Hark! What's uat?"

" That's the result, I expect," said my brother- in-law.

We drew up the blind and opened the window. The moon was shining brightly, and threw the monstrous shadow of the Cathedral very blackly upon the untrodden snow of the peaceful Close. Through the clear night air came the sound of frenzied cheering.

"That's it, right enough," said Gerald. "I wonder if you've got the chuck, my bonny boy."

" Ugh ! It is cold ! Come in," said Kitty.

We shut the window, drew down the blind, returned to the fire, and waited. Dolly joined us now, and Kitty vanished to sit by Phillis. We waited on. Somehow it never occurred to us to send downstairs for news. I suppose there are times when the human craving for sensation is sated. We sat and waited.

At last the door opened, and, as I expected, Robin entered. He looked like a man who has not been to bed for a week. He shut the door softly behind him – evidently he feared he might be entering a house of mourning – and surveyed us for a moment without speaking. I knew what was in his mind. Then he said –

"We have lost."

I stood up.

"On the contrary," I replied, " we have won."

In a bound Robin was on the hearth-rug, gripping my hand with his. (His other had somehow got hold of one of Dolly's, and I remember wondering if he was hurting her as much as me.)

"You mean it?" he roared.

"I do. She is sleeping like a lamb."

" Oh, man, I'm just glad 1 What does *anything* matter after that ? "

Then we sat down and smiled upon each other largely and vacuously. We were all a little unstrung that night, I think. After all, it seems rather unreasonable to lavish one's time, labour, and money on an electoral contest, and then laugh when you lose, and say it doesn't matter, just because a child isn't going to die. Oh, I am glad Mr Cash was not there!

" But I must tell you what happened when the result was read out," said Robin. " It was a near thing – a majority of twenty-seven. (I don't think it is worth while to ask for a recount: everything was done very carefully.) When the figures went up there was the usual hullabaloo "

"We heard it, thanks," said Gerald.

"And presently Stridge stepped out on to the balcony and bowed his acknowledgments. There was a lot more yelling and horn-blowing, and then they began to cry out for Inglethwaite."

"Naturally. Yes?"

"They were quiet at last, and Stridge got his speech in. He talked the usual blethers about having struck a blow that night that would ring through England, – just what *you* would have had to say if you had got in, in fact, – and *then* he went on, the old sumph, to Bay that for reasons best known to himself his *honourable* opponent had seen fit to withhold his presence from them that night, and he begged leave to add that he considered that a man, even though he knew he *was* going to be beaten, ought to have the pluck to come and face the music."

" Mangy bounder !" remarked my brother-in- law dispassionately.

" Oh, I was just raging!" continued Robin. " The people of course yelled themselves hoarse; and Stridge was going on to rub it into you, when I stepped on to the balcony beside him – I had been standing just inside the window – and I put my hand on Stridge's fat shoulder and I pulled him back a wee thing, and I roared –

"' Gentlemen, will you not let me say a word for Mr Inglethwaite ?'"

Dolly's eyes began to blaze, and I saw her lips part in anticipation.

" There was a tremendous uproar then," Robin went on with relish. " The folk howled to Stridge to put me over the balcony "

"I wish he had tried!" said Gerald with simple fervour.

M And other folk cried to me to go on. They knew there must be some explanation of your absence. I just stood there and let them roar. Inside the room there was a fine commotion; and with the tail of my eye I could see Cash hurrying round explaining to them what I wanted to say. (He has his points, Cash!) Then at last, as the noise got worse and worse, I put my mouth to Stridge's ear and bellowed that he would regret it all his life if he didn't let me say what I had to say, and that he would be grateful to me afterwards, and all that. He is a decent old buffer, really, and he was evidently impressed with what I said "

" I should like to know exactly what you did say, Robin," I interpolated.

"Never mind just now. Anyhow, he turned and clambered back into the room, and left me with the crowd. They were soon quiet, and I just told them."

Robin leaned back in his chair.

"Told them *what?*" came from all parts of the room.

But Robin had become suddenly and maddeningly Caledonian again.

"I just told them about Philly," he said.

"What else could I do? It wasn't like telling them during the election. That would have been an appeal to the gallery for votes. Thie was just common justice to you. Anyhow, they quite quietened down after that."

And that was all the report that its author ever gave us of a speech which, in the space of four minutes, turned a half-maddened election mob into a silent, a sympathetic, and (I heard afterwards) a deeply moved body of sober human beings.

" What happened next ?" asked Kitty, who had rejoined us. (Phillis was still sleeping sweetly, she said.)

" After that I hauled old Stridge on to the balcony again and gave him a congratulatory hand-shake, *coram populo,* on your behalf. Then I retired and slipped out by a back way and came here. Stridge was in full eruption again when I left "

Dolly held up her hand.

" What is that curious noise ? " she said.

" It's outside," said Kitty.

Gerald went to the window and lifted the blind. Then he turned to us.

"I say," he said in an unusual voice, "come here a minute."

We drew up the blind and surveyed the scene before us.

Two minutes before the moon had shone upon an untrodden expanse of snow. Now the Close was black with people. There must have been two or three thousand. They stood there in the gleaming moonlight, silent, motionless, like an army of phantoms. At their head and forefront – I could see the moonlight glitter on his watch-chain, which lay in a most favourable position for lunar reflection – stood the newly elected Member for Stoneleigh, Mr Alderman Stridge.

Simultaneously there was a knock at the door, and the hall-porter of the hotel appeared.

" Mr Stridge's compliments, sir, and he would like to have a word with you."

" Go down quickly, Adrian," said Kitty anxiously. "They'll wake Philly!"

I descended without a word, and passed out into the Close from a French window on the ground floor.

I glanced up in the direction of our rooms and noticed that my party were standing on the balcony outside the sitting-room. I could see Kitty's anxious face. But she need have had no fear.

Mr Stridge advanced towards me, silk hat in hand. Behind him stood a variety of Stone- leigh worthies, and I had time to notice that the group was composed of an indiscriminate mixture of friends and foes.

" Mr Inglethwaite, sir," said Stridge, " I should like to shake you by the hand."

He did so, as did a few of those immediately around us, in perfect silence. I wondered what was coming.

" That is all, sir," said Stridge simply, and not without a certain dignity. " We shall move off now. We did you a wrong to-night, and we all of us " – he indicated the motionless multitude with a sweep of his hand – " agreed to come here in silence, just for a moment, as an indication of our sympathy and – respect."

I was unable to speak, which was not altogether surprising. There was something overwhelming about the dumb kindness of it all, – three thousand excited folk holding themselves in for fear of disturbing a sick child, – and I merely shook Stridge's hand again.

However, I found my voice at last.

" Mr Stridge," I said, " there is only one thing I will say in response to your kindness, but I think it is the one thing most calculated toreward you all for it. To-night my little girl's illness took a favourable turn. She is now fast asleep, and practically out of danger."

I saw a great ripple pass over the crowd, like a breeze over a cornfield, as the news sped from mouth to mouth. Both Stridge's great hands were on my shoulders.

" Good lad 1" he said. " Good lad !"

He patted my shoulders again, and then, as if struck by a sudden idea, he turned and whispered a direction to his lieutenants. I overheard the words " Market Square," and " A good half mile away." Once more the wave passed over the cornfield, and without a sound the great concourse turned to the left and streamed away over the trampled snow, leaving me standing bareheaded on the steps of the French window, almost directly below the spot where the unconscious little object of all this consideration lay fast asleep.

I returned to the group on the balcony. They had heard most of the conversation, and Kitty was unaffectedly dabbing her eyes.

" Well, let us get in out of the cold," I said, suddenly cheerful and brisk. " I want my supper."

" Wait a moment," said Kobin, " I don't think

everything is quite over yet. What is that? Listen!"

From the direction of the Market Square came the shouts of a great multitude. Cheer upon cheer floated up to the starry heavens. The roars that had greeted the declaration of the poll were nothing to these. There was a united ring about them that had been lacking in the others. It was like one whole-hearted many- headed giant letting off steam.

"A-a-ht" said Kitty.

10

SECTION 10

CHAPTER SEVENTEEN.
IN WHICH ALL'S BIGHT WITH THE WORLD.

After that we became suddenly conscious of our bodily wants, and clamoured for supper.

It was long after midnight, and most of the hotel servants had gone to bed. But one waiter of political leanings, who had been an enthusiastic witness of the proceedings in the Close, stood by us nobly. He laid a table in the sitting-room. He materialised a cold turkey, a brown loaf, and some tomatoes; and he even achieved table-napkins. Gerald and Donkin on their part disappeared into the nether regions, and returned bearing mince - pies and cider. Some one else found champagne and opened it; and in a quarter of an hour we were left to ourselves by the benignant waiter round a comfortably loaded table, in a snug room with the fire burning and the curtains drawn.

It was an eccentric kind of meal, for every one was overflowing with a sort of reactionary hilarity; and everybody called everybody else " old man" or " my dear," and I was compelled to manipulate my food with my left hand owing to the fact that my wife insisted on clinging tightly to my right. The only times I got a really satisfactory mouthful were when ehe slipped out of the room to see how her daughter was sleeping.

As the meal progressed, I began to note the exceedingly domestic and intimate manner in which we were seated round the table, which was small and circular. Kitty and I sat together; then, on our right, came Dicky and Dilly, then Gerald and Donkin, each partially obscured from view by a bottle of cider about the size of an Indian club; and Dolly and Robin completed the circle.

The party comported themselves variously. Kitty and I said little. We were utterly-tired and dumbly thankful, and had no desira to contribute greatly to the conversation; but we turned and looked at one another in a contented sort of way at times. Dicky and Dilly were still sufficiently newly married to be more or less independent of other people's society. and they kept up a continuous undercurrent of lover-like confidences and playful nothings all the time. Gerald, upon whom solid food seemed to have the effect that undiluted alcohol has upon ordinary folk, was stentoriously engaged with Mr Donkin in what a student of *Paley's Evidences* would have described as "A Contest of Opposite Improbabilities" concerning his election experiences.

Lastly, I turned to Dolly and Robin. Dolly's splendid vitality has stood her in good stead during the last twenty-four hours, and this, combined with the present flood-tide of joyous relief, made it hard to believe that she had spent a day and a night of labour and anxiety. She was much more silent than usual, but her face was flushed and happy, and somehow I was reminded of the time when I had watched her greeting the dawn on the morning after Dilly's wedding. Robin, with the look of a man who has a hard day's work behind him, a full meal inside him, and a sound night's sleep before him – and what three greater blessings, could a man ask for himself? – sat beside her, smiling largely and restfully on the company around him.

Suddenly Dicky made an announcement).

"There is one more bottle," he said. "Come on, let's buzz it!"

He opened the champagne in a highly professional manner and filled up our glasses. Gerald and Donkin declined, but helped themselves to fresh jorums of cider.

Then there was a little pause, and we all felt that some one ought to make a speech or propose a toast.

" Shall we drink some healths ?" proposed Dilly.

There was a chorus of assent.

"We will each propose one," I said, "right round the table in turn. Ladies first! Yours, Kitty? I suppose it will be Philly – eh?"

Kitty nodded.

"Ladies and gentlemen," I announced, "you are asked to drink to the speedy recovery of Miss Phillis Inglethwaite. This toast is proposed by her mother, and seconded by her father."

The toast was drunk with all sincerity, but soberly, as befitted.

"Now, Dilly," I said, when we were ready again.

Dilly whispered something to her husband, which was received by that gentleman with a modest and deprecatory cough, coupled with an urgent request that his wife would chuck it.

"He won't announce my toast for me," explained Duly, turning to us – " he's too shy, poor dear! – so I'll do it myself. Ladies and gentlemen, the toast is – Dicky !"

Dicky's health was drunk with cheers and laughter, and Dilly completed its subject's confusion by kissing him.

" Now, Dolly !" said every one.

" Not yet!" said Dolly. " Gerald and Moke are the next pair. Gerald must act lady, and think of a toast."

Master Gerald, hastily bolting a solid mass of mince-pie – one could almost follow the course of its descent – cheerfully complied.

"All right," he said; "I think I'll drink the health of old Moke himself. He's not much to look at, but he's a good sort. I shan't kiss him, though, Dilly. And," he added, " I think he had better drink mine too. He looks thirsty. Come on, sonny – no heeltaps!"

He elaborately linked arms with the now comatose Donkin, and each thereupon absorbed, without drawing breath, about a pint of cider apiece. After that, with a passing admonition to his friend not to burst, my brother-in-law returned to his repast.

So far, the toasts had all been of a most conventional and inevitable character. Now, automatically but a little tactlessly, we all turned to see what Dolly and Robin were going to do. From the standpoint of the last two toasts they were certainly in a rather delicate position.

" Come on, you two!" commanded Gerald. " Do something ! Make a spring !"

Robin took up his glass of champagne and turned rather inquiringly to Dolly.

Without a word she linked her arm in his, and they drank together.

" Oh, come, I say, that's not fair! Whose health were you drinking, Robin, old man ?" inquired the tactless Dicky.

" I was drinking to the future Mrs Fordyce – whoever she may be !" said Robin, obviously apologetic at being unable to think of anything more sparkling.

"Whose health were *you* drinking, Dolly?" yelled Gerald, with much enjoyment.

Then Dolly did a startling thing.

Robin's hand lay resting on the table beside her. Into it she deliberately slipped her own; and then gazed – flushed and defiant, but proud and smiling – round a circle composed entirelyof faces belonging to people suffering from the gapes.

I glanced at Robin. He looked perfectly dumfounded, but I saw his hand close automatically round Dolly's fingers, and I saw, too, her pink nails go white under the pressure.

But Dolly seemed to feel no pain. On the contrary, she continued to smile upon us. Then, bowing her head quickly, before any of us realised what she would be at, she lightly kissed the great hand which imprisoned her own. Then she looked up again, with glistening eyes.

" There !" she said. " *Now* you know !"

Our breath came back, and the spellbound silence was broken.

"Dolly!" said Kitty.

"My *dear!"* said Dilly.

"What – *ho!"* drawled Dicky.

But it was Gerald who rounded off the situation. He was standing on the table by this time.

" Three cheers for Dolly and Robin!" he roared.

We gave them, with full throats. (Fortunately we were a long way from Phillis's room.)

After that we all sat down again, feeling a little awkward, as people do when they have

taken the lid off their private feelings for a moment. Finally Kitty led off with –

"But, Dolly, dear, why didn't you tell us? When was it?"

"I didn't tell you before," said Dolly composedly, "because it has only just happened – this moment."

"Only this moment? But "

" Do you mean to say he hasn't *asked* you ? Oh "

" Are you asking *him f* "

The questions came simultaneously from all parts of the table; horribly inquisitive, some of them; but then the thing had been so frankly and deliberately done, that we knew Dolly wanted to explain everything to us there and then.

" I'll tell you," said Dolly, after silence had been restored by the fact that Gerald had shouted us all down and then stopped himself. "Robin told' me – well – something, six months ago, the night after Dilly's wedding, at the dance "

" That *was* why you locked the door, then," I said involuntarily.

Both Robin and Dolly turned upon me in real amazement. But I saw that this side-issue would interrupt the story.

" Never mind!" I said. " Go on! I'll explain afterwards."

"Well," continued Dolly, "he said to me – may I tell them, Robin?" She turned to the man beside her with a pretty air of deference. Robin, who up to this point had sat like a graven image, inclined his head, and Dolly proceeded –

" I have never told anybody about this – except Dilly, of course."

" I've got the letter still," said Dilly.

"Robin told me," Dolly went on, "that he wasn't going to ask me to marry him at present, because he had some childish idea – it is perfectly *idiotic* to think of; but – he thought he wasn't quite – well, *good* enough for me!"

"What rot!" said Dicky.

"Muck!" observed Gerald.

" But he said that he would ask me properly later on, as soon as he considered that he *was* good enough," continued Dolly. "And as he still seems to think," she concluded with more animation, " that he is not quite up to standard, it occurred to me to-night, as we were all here in a jolly little party, to notify him that he *is*. So I did. That's all. Robin, you are hurting my hand 1"

Robin relaxed his grip at last, and remorsefully surveyed the bloodless fingers that lay in his palm. Then, with a rather shamefaced look all round the table, as much as to say – " I should like fine to restrain myself from doing this before you all, but I *can't!*" – he bent his head and kissed them in his turn.

And that was how Robin and Dolly plighted their troth at last – openly, without shame, and for all to see.

Robin and I lingered at the turning of a passage, lit only by our two flickering bedroom candles.

" Well, we can't complain of having had an uneventful day," I said.

" I'm sorry we didn't scrape other twenty- eight votes," said Robin characteristically.

" Never mind!" I said. " I shall be none the worse of a holiday for a year or two. If you will kindly take Dolly *off* our hands as quickly as possible" – he caught his breath at that – " Kitty and I and Phillis will go a trip round the world together. Then I'll come home and fight a by-election, perhaps."

" Meanwhile," said Robin, " you will be having no further need of a private secretary."

"Pih afraid not," I said. The fact had been tugging at my conscience for the last two hours. "And that raises another question. What are you two going to live on?"

" Champion wants me," said Robin. " He has offered me the post of Secretary to that Royal Commission of which he has been appointed Chairman. It is a fine opening."

" I should think it was!" I said with wholehearted joy. " Good luck to you, Robin !
"

" Thank you !" said Robin. " Still," he added, as he turned to go, " I wish I could have found you twenty-eight more votes."

"Between ourselves," I said, "I don't mind very much. I am not the right man for this constituency. It has outgrown me. I have not the knack of handling a big crowd. What I want is a fine old crusted uuprogressive seat, where I shan't constantly be compelled to drop my departmental work and rush down to propitiate my supporters with untruthful harangues. I'm a square peg here. Now, if they had wanted a really fit and proper candidate for this Parliamentary Division, Robin, they ought to have approached *you.*"

" Och!" said Robin carelessly, " they did – a month ago! Good night!" 310

CHAPTER EIGHTEEN.

A PROPHET IN HIS OWN COUNTBT.

An old woman in a white mutch stands at the door of a farmhouse in a Scottish glen. Her face is wrinkled, and her dim eyes are peering down the track which leads from the steading to the pasture. Being apparently unable to focus what she wants to see she adjusts a pair of spectacles.

This action brings into her range of vision a distant figure which is engaged in shepherding a herd of passive but resisting cows through a gap in the dyke. It is a slow business, but the procession gradually nears home; and when the man at the helm succeeds in steering his sauntering charges safely between the Scylla of a hay-rick and the Charybdis of the burn, the old lady takes off" her spectacles and relaxes her vigilance.

When she looks again, though, she breaksinto an exclamation of dismay. The leaders of the straggling procession have safely reached the door of the byre close by; but one frisky young cow, suddenly swerving through an open gate, breaks away down a sloping field of turnips at a lumbering gallop. The herdsman is out of sight round a bend in the road.

" The feckless body!" observes the old lady bitterly. Then she raises her voice.

"Elspeth!"

A reply comes from within the dairy.

" Ay, mem ?"

"You'll need tae leave the butter and help Master Robert. He's no hand with the kye. He's let Heatherbell intill the neeps. And the maister is away at "

With a muffled " Maircy me !" a heated young woman shoots out of a side door and proceeds at the double to the assistance of the incompetent cow-herd.

At length the animals are rounded up into the byre, and Elspeth proceeds with the milking.

Meanwhile Master Robert, " the feckless body," stands in a rather apprehensive attitude before the old lady. He is a huge man of about forty-five. He is clean-shaven, and he has humorous grey eyes and dark hair. Despitehis homespun attire, he looks more like a leader of men than a driver of cattle.

"Robin Fordyce," says the old lady severely, "what garred ye loose Heatherbell in among the neeps.

" I'm sorry, mother. But I met Jean M'Taggart in the road, and – we stopped for a bit crack."

The old lady surveys her son witheringly over her glasses.

" Dandering wi' Jean M'Taggart at your time of life ! I'll sort Jean M'Taggart when I see her. It's jist like her tae try and draw a lad from his duty. And you! A married man these fifteen years! 'Deed, and it's tune yon lady wife of yours cam' here from London, tae pit a hand on you."

The big man's penitent face lights up with sudden enthusiasm.

"She is coming to-morrow!" he roars exultantly.

" Aye, you may pretend tae be glad! But she shall hear aboot Jean M'Taggart all the same," replies the old lady.

This, of course, is a tremendous joke, and the inquisition is suspended while mother and son chuckle deeply at the idea of Dolly's desperate jealousy. Suddenly Mrs Fordyce breaks off to ask a question.

"Did ye mind tae shut the gate of the west field?"

Robin thinks, and then raises clenched hands to heaven in an agony of remorse.

His mother groans in a resigned sort of way.

" Run!" she says, " or ye'll hae all the sheep oot in the road! Get them back, and I'll no' tel l David on ye !"

Her son bounds away down the 'slope, but a further command pursues him.

" An' come back soon! I'll no' be getting you tae mysel' over much after – to-morrow !"

She sits down again in her chair outside the door in the afternoon sun; for she is getting infirm now, and cannot stand up for long. With an indulgent sigh she surveys the flying figure of the Right Honourable Sir Robert Chalmers Fordyce, Privy Councillor and Secretary of State, as he frantically endeavours to overtake and head off three staid ewes, who, having strayed through the open gate, have just decided upon a walking excursion to London.

"A good lad!" she murmurs contentedly. " A good lad, and a good son; and dae'n' weel. But – he's no' just David. It was always David that had the heid on him."

A prophet, we know, has no honour in his own country. Fortunately some prophets prefer that this should be the case.

The am.

This book should be returned to the Library on or before the last date stamped below.

A fine of five cents a day is incurred by retaining it beyond the specified time.

Please return promptly.

,-1

itkll ..

= OPR17'ii

Lightning Source UK Ltd.
Milton Keynes UK
UKOW051346120412

190592UK00002B/22/P